Le Jardin Retrouvé

The Music of Frederic Mompou 1893-1987

by

Wilfrid Mellers

With illustrations by
ROBIN HILDYARD

We know that we have our childhood with us always, because it must be as Saint Augustine has written: if it were not here, wither would it have gone?
EVAN S. CONELL: Notes from a bottle found on the beach at Carmel.

Travis & Emery

Wilfrid Mellers : Le Jardin Retrouvé
The Music of Frederic Mompou

First published by The Fairfax Press 1987.

Republished Travis & Emery 2007.

© Wilfrid Mellers 1987.

ACKNOWLEDGEMENTS
The musical examples have been reproduced by kind permission of Editions Max Esch, Paris, Editions Heugel S.A., Paris, editions Salabert, Paris and Union Musical Española S.A. Madrid / United Music Publishers Ltd.

Published by
Travis & Emery Music Bookshop
17 Cecil Court, London, WC2N 4EZ, United Kingdom.
(+44) 20 7240 2129
neworders@travis-and-emery.com

Hardback: ISBN10: 1-904331-24-6   ISBN13: 978-1904331-24-7
Paperback: ISBN10: 1-904331-25-4   ISBN13: 978-1904331-25-4

To
FREDERICK FULLER
*whose magical singing revealed the
major magic of Mompou's minor muse.*

CONTENTS

	Prelude	page 1
I	Spain and Europe, Tradition and Mompou	4
II	Mompou's Apprenticeship: a Path through the Garden	26
III	Mompou, Bells and Spells	36
IV	Mompou's *Ludi Puerorum*	59
V	Mompou as Peasant Plus	80
VI	Mompou and 'Europe', Adolescence and Art	100
VII	Mompou, the Church, and *La Soledad Sonora*	115
	Postlude	136

Prelude

> I salute you in your
> Garden State!
> You taught us to
> scrape all the leaves off the Bottom of the Barrel.
> JONATHAN WILLIAMS

FREDERIC MOMPOU died in 1987 at the age of ninety-four. He was thus a near-contemporary of Spanish-Catalan artists – Picasso, Miró, Casals – who attained heights in their respective realms, and of a Catalan composer, Roberto Gerhard, who deservedly became a figure of European renown. Mompou himself can make no claim to Greatness. Although he composed with discreet consistency over three quarters of a century, he produced little music and that almost exclusively in small forms – brief piano pieces and songs for voice and piano, with a sprinkling of liturgical works for his Roman Church.

Even so, the appeal of Mompou's music has been disproportionate to its minimal means. The word most often used to describe this appeal is 'haunting': which is appropriate, because the curiously timeless music has magical properties. Mompou has called himself a composer of *recommencement*. Discarding many of the techniques of a Europe grown weary if not moribund, he has sought renewal in pre-historical spells, charms and incantations; in the sung and danced games of children; in religious rites and secular festivities of an indigenous folk culture; and to a lesser degree in memories of his Church as it may have been in its medieval and early Renaissance heyday. Living in Paris for more than twenty years, he found hints towards his *renouvellement* in the sophisticated

Le Jardin Retrouvé

Debussy and Ravel; in another and very different minimalist, Erik Satie; and in another sophisticated Parisian exile from a remote (partially) peasant world, Frédéric Chopin. Yet Mompou's music is unlike theirs or anyone's; the potency of his modest muse depends on its being at once unique and also universal, in the sense that we all harbour a measure of Mompou's longing for the Forgotten Garden of childhood wherein the heart was, or seemed to be, whole, in the spring of the year. This affects us the more deeply the more 'pluralistically' exacerbated our mechanized civilization grows.

Mompou has never lacked acolytes and the strength of his fragility is sufficient to encourage increase in their numbers. His earliest music, composed when he was a boy of sixteen or seventeen, retains its vernality undimmed; his latest music, created during his eighties, is recognizably that of the same boy-man, though it has grown more intensely exiguous as it has become more religiously, perhaps mystically, hermetic. That such minimal *material* – the jargon word is in his case singularly inappropriate – has made so durable an impact suggests that it must be of remarkable quality.

At this point a personal note, from another man now old if less old than Mompou, may be relevant. The earliest composition to which I still own is called *The Forgotten Garden:* a cantata for tenor and string quartet setting a poem about Eden by the 17th century Nature mystic, Henry Vaughan. Throughout the years since 1945, the theme has been recurrent in my music, and for that matter in my writings also. So I pay this tribute as one old Edenicist to another. Vaughan, admitting to the Fall, exclaimed

> But ah! my soule, with too much Staye
> Is drunke, and Staggers in the way.
> Some men a Forward Motion love
> But I by Backward Steps would move,
> And when this Dust falls to the Urne
> In that state I came returne.
>
> (SILEX SCINTILLANS 1655)

Prelude

Mompou too thus admitted to 'regression', and both as boy and as grown man seems precariously to have preserved a vision of those 'happy early days when I Shined in my Angel Infancy'. To him is appropriate the more philosophical, rather than theological, formulation of Gertrude Stein, who has so often revealed the wisdom within the prattle of babes and sucklings:

> There are some when they feel it inside them that it has been with them that there was once so very little of them, that they were a baby, helpless and no conscious feeling in them, that they knew nothing then when they were kissed and dandled and fixed by others who knew them when they could know nothing inside them or around them, some get from all this that once surely happened to them to that which was then every bit that was then them, there are some when they feel it later inside them that they were such once and that was all there was of them then, there are some who have from such a knowing an uncertain curious kind of feeling in them that their having been so little once and knowing nothing makes it all a broken world for them that they have made inside them, kills for them that everlasting feeling; and they spend their life in many ways, and always they are trying to make for themselves a new everlasting feeling.
> (A LONG GAY BOOK 1909–1912)

Oliver Sheldon House, Aldwark, York
September 28 1987

Thanks are due to the book's dedicatee, Frederick Fuller, for invaluable linguistic and other corrections to the original ms.

I

Spain and Europe, Tradition and Mompou

> Scratch a Spaniard and you find a Saracen. And all this is very important with what I have been saying about the peaceful oriental penetration into European culture or rather the tendency for this generation that is the twentieth century to be no longer European perhaps because Europe is finished.
>
> GERTRUDE STEIN

> Mudar costumbre a par de Muerte.
>
> SPANISH PROVERB

FREDERIC MOMPOU believed himself to be a composer of *recommencement:* of the Eternal Return by way of childhood, spells, magic and incantation. Before we explore how his magic is musically manifest, we must ask why such a composer appeared in Spain, and particularly in Catalonia, rather than elsewhere. The answer is geographical and historical as well as cultural. Geographically, Spain is 'out on a limb', cut off from the rest of Europe by the Pyrenees, a barrier as much psychological as physical. Her north eastern provinces are thus segregated from France, her closest neighbour; while in the south she looks away from Europe towards Africa and the dark forces of the Infidel. As early as 711 southern Spain was invaded by the Moors, who rapidly spread north. Not until 1492 was Spain recaptured by and for Spaniards; and Moorish power remained pervasive for at least another hundred years. The infidel was, however, far from barbaric. The distinctive quality of Spanish culture has always been that her legacy of (classical)

Spain and Europe, Tradition and Mompou

Roman civilization and of 'Roman' Christianity fused richly and imperceptibly with Moslem traditions which, in poetry, music, visual arts, science, mathematics and theology were of high sophistication, if alien, in their oriental atemporality, to long cherished assumptions of Roman Law and of Western Church and State. Such a synthesis of age-old, pre-Christian spiritual and intellectual concepts with those of the West was abetted by Spain's geographical position, which enabled her to resist mutability. Nor was this restricted to southern regions, for in the north Catalans and Basques had been from prehistoric times tinged with Berber blood. During Spain's Middle Ages and early Renaissance Christians worked in re-creative harmony with Moslems, Sephardic Jews and Berbers, attaining artistic heights in part dependent on her isolation from the mainland. The intrusion of a potent popular culture associated with alien gypsies intensified this darkness within, yet also beyond, Christian tradition.

Culturally, the Moorish-Christian, Eastern-Western alliance worked well during Spain's Middle Ages and Renaissance. Politically, however, it was a different story, for no people enjoys being a subject race. The Christian *reconquista* completed in the late 15th century spelled the decline of Arabic influence, yet proved in the process how Moslem domination had paradoxically strengthened the Spaniard's European Catholicism. Their conservatism and pride sprang from a desperate adherence to what, having once been lost, might be lost again. The political reinforced the religious motive; national unification grew obsessive when it could be so patently threatened. Spanish culture embraced Moors and Muslims while at the same time unity against the infidel became a basic motivation of the Spanish character.

After Spain's Golden Century, she declined. The Inquisition is usually related to, even blamed for, this: not so much because of its horror – it was no less horrid elsewhere – as because of its durability. It erupted out of anger, demanding revenge on an alien culture; it went on and on out of fear: terror lest the Old

Le Jardin Retrouvé

World might disappear, leaving chaos in its place. Spain became an obstructionist backwater. From this sprang *El Sentimiento Trágico de la Vida* of which Unamuno wrote in the book published under that title in 1913. The Spaniard and his country are alike 'tragic' because they remain medieval in spirit, having passed through the Renaissance, Reformation and Revolution with no more than superficial effect. Spanish Quixotism is the 'despairing struggle of the Middle Ages against the Renaissance'; and even in our own day the Civil War was 'won' by the Old Guard which, with Christian spirituality now in abeyance, imposed its will through political fanaticism as much as religious bigotry. Today, Church and State are alike tarnished; there has been little positive resurgence of Spanish social pride or religious fervour. With a few exceptions – Picasso, Miró, Lorca – her most distinguished artists are minor, even mini. Frederic Mompou is a classic example.

Throughout the centuries the story of Spanish music naturally parallels her religious, social and political evolution. Spanish separatism and conservatism mean that her folk musics, rich as they are in springing from pre-historic roots, have been more than usually resistant to the winds of chance and to corruption by industrial and commercial pressures. Southern folk musics, sun-baked, relished the filigree of Moorish decoration; northern folk musics tended to a gentler lyricism analogous to that of Provence. Both southern eroticism and northern spirituality acquired a typically Spanish ardour, reinforced in interaction with the wilder musics of gypsy aliens, who infiltrated into western Europe between the mid-thirteenth and the mid-sixteenth centuries. Musically, their flamenco – or at least the Andalusian version of it – has become a recipe for Instant Hispanicism for tourists, though the commercialized model has tenuous connections with the real thing. That obscurity should surround the music of so obscure a race is appropriate; even the word flamenco is etymologically confused. It is sometimes derived from Fleming – tawny-skinned Beethoven was youthfully nicknamed the Fleming or the Gypsy; but it may also be

Spain and Europe, Tradition and Mompou

related to the Arabic *fellah mangu*, meaning to sing, while the romany word *Flaman*, signifying bold and bright, is still in use. Whatever the confusion, there is no doubt about the gypsies' advent from the Orient, nor about their contact and communion with Arabs and Jews already established in Spain; Spanish music would not be what it is had not the filigreed ornamentation, irregular rhythms and acrid sonorities of Moorish and Sephardic cantillation been tinged with the gypsies' duskier fire. A decree of Charles V in Toledo, dated May 24 1539, specifically dubbed them *egyptani gitani*.

In culturally segregated Spain, during the Middle Ages, the inter-relation of folk with art traditions was even closer than it was in the rest of 'civilized' Europe. This is evident in the several collections of religious monodies that have survived: most impressively in the four hundred *Cantigas de Santa Maria* garnered together, and perhaps in part composed by, Alfonso X (1230–1280), King of Castile and Leon. Justifiably nicknamed El Sabio, he was a man of high cultivation in poetry, music and the visual arts and, being interested and probably trained in mathematics and science, was also known as the Astronomer. That art may override anthropological and geographical barriers was demonstrated at his brilliant court, at which Christians, Moslems and Jews worked amicably together, under Christian rule. Many Arabs, known as *mudejares*, earned distinction as architects, doctors, botanists, linguisticians and musicians; and the musicians readily absorbed Christian plainsong and troubadour monody into their native musical conventions, Arabic and European instruments being used impartially. The texts of the Cantigas, mostly hymns of praise to the Virgin Mary, extolling her deeds and the miracles performed in her name, were in the Galician language rather than in Latin. Alfonso chose Galician – the language of the northern province of Leon – because a poetic and theological tradition already flourished there, associated with the spiritual centre of St. James's tomb at Santiago de Compostela, whither pilgrims had long resorted as refuge from Islamic oppression. Galician, a

Le Jardin Retrouvé

language related to Portuguese, was regarded by Alfonso as a 'people's tongue', through which the treasures of a hermetic court might be disseminated.

Of course the cantigas are not in fact popular music; both verbally and musically they are constructed on elaborate principles derived from Provençal troubadour poetry and music, Provence being the nub of medieval civilization. Even so, it is significant that the cantigas efface boundaries between the sacred and the secular. There is little distinction between their homage to the Virgin Mary – a Mother of God also personified as a flesh and blood woman – and the troubadours' celebration of an earthly mistress who, being beyond wedlock (usually because married to someone else), is identified with the Eternal Beloved: a metaphysical ideal rather than a physical reality. In assembling these songs Alfonso considered himself an heir to King David: an Orphic singer healing mental and bodily wounds through spiritual devotion. Describing himself as 'troubadour of the Virgin Mary', he makes heart-easing melodies which resemble those of the Provençal troubadour in moving by plainsong-like steps, minor thirds and fourths, in flexibly rhythmed contours of grace and purity. They sound – though this may be to us now rather than to them then – wistful, as though aware of disparity between spiritual ideality and the brute facts of fallen nature. At the same time earthy corporeality is not evaded, creeping in by the back door of the folk culture. Arabian influence works in both directions, aspiring to spirituality in winging arabesques, emphasizing physicality through the raucous penetration of arabic melody instruments and the continuity of oriental percussion. Singing styles must have been no less equivocal, poised between West and East.

We cannot know precisely how the cantigas were sung and played, if played they were. The exquisite manuscripts notate pitch but not rhythm, and give no indication of instrumentation. We may speculate as to how the music sounded, on the evidence of Christian-Arabic singing styles still extant, and on the basis of visual iconography which shows both Western and

Spain and Europe, Tradition and Mompou

Eastern percussion instruments being employed, along with pipes and plucked and bowed strings presumably acting as drones or in primitive heterophony. Such reconstructions as have been attempted – notably by Thomas Binkley with the Schola Cantorum Basiliensis – are enthralling enough, in their fusion of high sophistication with naivety, momentarily to convince, even if their premises should prove untenable. The music sounds in tune with us today – especially with some aspects of 'progressive' (which in a sense is regressive) pop music. That there is a link with Mompou *can* be proven, since he quotes melodies from the cantigas, and it's difficult to tell where quotation stops and individual creation takes over.

The cantigas of S. Alonso may be the most profoundly Spanish contribution to musical culture. After the slow conquest of the Muslims and the expulsion of the Jews, the Spanish Renaissance made some mark on the outside world: as is allegorized by Columbus's discovery of a New World. Queen Isabella's motto of 'One God, One King, One Law' was a positive manifestation of the patriotic and religious zeal for unification: which had its negative complement in political oppression and religious persecution. At this time – the late 15th and early 16th century – power-consciousness encouraged contact with 'Europe', the more so because of marital alliances between Spain and France and mercantile relationships with the Netherlands; La Rue, Agricola and Ockeghem were merely a few of the foreign composers who had court or ecclesiastical appointments in Spain. Spanish Renaissance music, 'law'-dominated, more extremely follows the general European pattern in being harmonic rather than monodic, and more metrically *ordered* than the music of the previous generations. True, some of the pieces collated between 1450 and 1515 for use at the court of Ferdinand and Isabella betray links with the past in that they are love songs addressed to a beloved liable to metamorphosis into the Virgin Mary, while others derive from the ancient tradition of balladic *romance*. Even so, it's interesting that the leading composer of the time, Juan del Encina

Le Jardin Retrouvé

(1468–1529), made infrequent use of his contrapuntal skill, favouring the *villancico*, literally meaning a rustic song, thereby creating a Spanish version of the Italian madrigal which remained for the most part homophonic, four-square in rhythm. Such chordally harmonized part songs inevitably merged into solo songs with lute, harp or guitar accompaniment. Only the amazing songs of the Sephardic Jews preserved, from the 14th into the 17th century, the old monody's intoxicating mingle of mystical ecstasy, filigreed eroticism, and peasant virility.

In Spanish Spain the new harmonic idiom was sturdily established by the mid-sixteenth century, to a degree in the densely textured, Flemish-style church music of a composer like Alfonso Mudarra (1520–1580), more obviously in the secular songs of a Luis Milan (1510–1560), which offered delightful relief from the rigour of the royal God, King and Law by dealing in the loves of common folk, alleviating patrician pride with earthiness, aristocratic finesse with gypsyish fire. Similar qualities function with greater artistic force in the music of the blind organist Antonio de Cabezón (1510–1560), who in his plainsong fancies imbued a superb contrapuntal technique with Spanish mystical fervour, while contemporaneously producing brilliantly corporeal *differencias* or variations on rural and urban pop tunes, equally effective on organ or on harpsichord. And the Spanish baroque organ for which Cabezón composed was a very special instrument. It would seem that people invent the instrument appropriate to their imaginative needs; no other European community built organs like the Spanish, capable of seraphic cantillation on the flutes, yet no less conducive to a nasal bravura recalling now the ferocity of flamenco singing, now the raucous wind-and-brass scoring of Iberian street bands. The Spanish synthesis of sexuality and mysticism, blood and death, reverberates, oblivious of social gentility, through the plangent, even cruel, sonorities of her ecclesiastical and civic organs, and is visually manifest in the famous *trompetas reales,* fanning in phallic if royal exuberance into the upper spaces of the buildings. This exhibitionism, no more than latent in Cabezón, becomes patent after his day – in, for instance, the harmonically tortuous, even 'crucified' music of Francisco Correa de Arrauxo (floreat 1600–1635), and in the high baroque ebullience of Johannis Cabanilles (1644–1712).

The apex to Spain's artistic Golden Age occurred in the late 16th and early 17th century, complementary to England's Elizabethan and Jacobean glory. Shakespeare, exploring the heights and depths of the human mind, is contemporary with Cervantes, and Salvador de Madariaga, in his book *Spain*, has a revealing paragraph contrasting Shakespeare's Hamlet with Cervantes' Don Quixote. Not for nothing have these two mythical characters become archetypal in popular consciousness. Hamlet is a would-be Faustian man of action immobilized by the introspection which is itself part of his need to think and to know; he is rendered impotent because, conscience-ridden, he is clever and moral enough to recognize that what he 'has' to do is an act that properly belongs to God alone. Don Quixote, on the other hand, has no difficulty in acting; indeed he acts blindly, at the behest of whims and of chivalric conventions to which he can no longer give intellectual, but only mythological, justification, so that his acts function in a void, to no public or even privately efficacious end. Between them, Hamlet and Don Quixote epitomize the English and Spanish 'ethos'. The one, in a forward-looking society, is called upon to sacrifice dreams in the interests of progress and moral responsibility; the other, in an ossifying society, substitutes dreams and memories for ends.

If musical parallels between Spain and England at the turn into the 17th century are less profound in implication than this comparison between Cervantes and Shakespeare, they certainly exist. The intrepid Dr. John Bull, investigating scholastic puzzles and enharmonic mysteries through the medium of (demonically possessed, some said) keyboard virtuosity, is a counterpart to the more virtuosic Spanish organists. The singing lutenist-composer John Dowland, confronting the darkness of Melancholy in a Hamlet-like introspection

Le Jardin Retrouvé

annealed by Platonic idealism, is the consummation of a long tradition Spanish in origin, since the lute (or vihuela), having been borrowed from Arabian sources, had combined with the vocal tradition of the villancico to create a rich literature of songs and instrumental dances. Although the greater maturity of the English lute school may be related to the fact that England was more 'progressive' at this key-point in history, she too was a turbulently divisive society: John Bull was a Catholic recusant who spent the last years of his life in exile at Antwerp (he may possibly have been a spy); John Dowland spent some years in malcontent at the Danish court of Elsinore. Even William Byrd, greatest and most many-sided of English composers, was equivocal: a Roman Catholic permitted to serve a Protestant Queen, creating his greatest music to Latin texts, for the Roman liturgy. The difference between Byrd and Spain's complement to him, Tomás Luis de Victoria (1548–1611), is significant: for whereas Byrd embraced every medium then available to a musician, Victoria restricted himself to vocal liturgical music for his Church. He was 'Roman' to the extent of spending much of his life in Rome, in the Church's service: a fact which does not compromise the profoundly Spanish quality of his inspiration. He writes for voices with the mellifluously Roman classicality of Palestrina, while achieving from his polyphony an intensity often compared to El Greco's Spanish-Greek-Byzantine distortion of Italian forms. Victoria's exploitation of contrasted vocal 'registers' – especially in his famous offices for the dead – may even suggest analogies with the sonorities of the Spanish baroque organ. The terror and ecstacy of the ritual bull-fight is not far below the surface.

During the course of the 17th century Spanish music followed the European pattern in being progressively secularized. Among many song collections produced at the court of Philip IV (1605–1665) the most illustrious are the Cancionero de Claudio de la Sablonara and the Libro de Tonos Humanos. Sablonara, a fairly prolific composer, was eclipsed in fame by Matero Romero (1575–1647), nicknamed 'Capitán' because of

Spain and Europe, Tradition and Mompou

his conspicious talents, and later by Juan Hidalgo (1612–1685), renowned alike as composer, harpist, harpsichordist and notary for the Inquisition. The villancicos of these men, succeeding to the tradition of Luis Milan, are short, earthy, rather aggressive in their folk-like virility: though secular in impulse, they were sometimes adapted to liturgical uses, taking priority over traditionally devotional music. Later in the century *tonos humanos* lost much of their sinew. Adapted to the stage in the popular theatre known as *zarzuela* – a Spanish complement to the Italian Commedia dell'Arte – they became a sung and danced pop music in which Spanish abrasiveness was mollified by the Italianate operatic lyricism that was to dominate Europe by the early 18th century. This evolution entailed a decline parallel to that undergone by British music during the same period, though the reasons for the two declensions were not parallel but opposite. Whereas England, in her progressive optimism, embraced the scientific and later industrial revolution in ways inimical to music, Spain was immobilized in defensive regression. Either way, native musical creativity withered. Foreigners – first Handel, then Mendelssohn and Spohr – took over English music; the Italian Scarlatti, settled in Spain, became more Spanish than the natives, attaining a vivacity that local composers, even the brilliant Soler, could not rival. A decade or so later another Italian, Luigi Boccherini, made Spain his homeland, producing quantities of music for the Infante Don Luis and the King himself. Though Boccherini didn't, like Scarlatti, become a vicarious Spanish composer he betrayed, in his permutations of the rococo Franco-Italianate-Austro idiom in which the court delighted, an Hispanicism deeper than 'local colour'. His string writing combines elegance with whiffs of gypsy fervour; in his guitar quintets he writes expertly for that highly idiosyncratic instrument, even incorporating a fandango as (in more than one sense) vulgarly insidious as Ravel's notorious *Bolero*.

This is a deliberate exercise in musical 'slumming' which doesn't radically affect Boccherini's Italianate-Austrian idiom.

Le Jardin Retrouvé

The same European stylization is adopted by the only native Spanish composer of the early 19th century distinguished by genius as well as talent. Juan Christostomo Arriaga was born in Bilbao, of a well-to-do family, in 1806; was playing in string quartets by the age of ten; and by fourteen had composed a couple of operas and a fair amount of other music both vocal and instrumental. Sent to study in Paris, the prodigy developed a technical finesse rivalling that of Mozart, to whom he was inevitably compared. In his twentieth year he died in Paris, burnt out by a 'galloping' consumption; one might say that, had he lived, the story of Spanish music would have been different; one might also say that the fact that he died so young is itself evidence of Spain's moribund condition. However that may be, one can certainly claim that his opera *Los esclavos felices,* of which the overture is still occasionally performed, yields nothing to the boy Mozart in effervescence and technical skill; while the three string quartets he produced in 1821–22, when he was seventeen, and still more the ambitious D minor symphony, add to technical expertise and lyrical animation an electrical charge that may owe something to his Iberian ancestry. These works can sustain comparison with youngish Mozart; the dazzlingly ferocious finale of the symphony even suggests young Beethoven 'the Fleming', though normally Arriaga's wit is less disruptive than Beethoven's, more boyishly Rossinian in its sense of fun. By the time of his death Arriaga had learned how to imbue his fusion of Italian theatrical and Austrian symphonic drama with a distinctive personal character. If this character has little or no national flavour – except possibly in the delightfully bucolic finale of the D minor quartet and the programmatic Pastorale of the E flat major quartet – that is because Arriaga has talent enough to be European without ceasing to be Spanish.

This works, given a composer of precocious genius; in the hands of routine practitioners, however, 19th century Spanish music became, in surrendering national identity, character*less* if colourful, whether in instrumental terms or in the popular

Spain and Europe, Tradition and Mompou

theatre. When national consciousness returned it was, in music as in politics, a self-conscious gesture. It is interesting – in view of Gertrude Stein's comments on Spain's 'Saracen' orientalism – that the first composer to popularize, even to commercialize, Spanish music in the world at large should have been a Russian, Glinka: who, having visited Spain in the eighteen-forties, produced the first 'musical picture postcards' of Spain in his *Spanish Overture* and *Night in Madrid*. Their vivid example inspired Rimsky-Korsakov to produce his more stream-lined *Spanish Capriccio:* from which point a succession of Frenchmen created the image still accepted by most concert-goers as Spanish music. Nor is the image altogether false: Lalo, creator of the *Fantasie Espagnole,* had Spanish blood in his veins; Bizet discovered in his Carmen the soul of Spain through the empathy of his precocious genius; Chabrier, Debussy and Ravel made music which, on no less authority than that of Manuel de Falla, was truer to Spain's heart than was the work of most contemporary nationalists.

Such being the state of affairs at the turn into the 20th century, it is hardly surprising that the few great Spanish artists in any medium migrated to Paris; as did the more interesting little ones, among them Mompou. This does not alter the fact that memories of the 'real' Spain still fired their muse. Indeed in voluntary exile their Spanishness became the more potent; they were more capable of embracing it in ideality than in fact. Perhaps Spain, geographically 'enclosed' and vigorously autonomous in her folk arts, had little need of Artists to assert her identity. Paradoxically, such artists as there were tended to look back nostalgically to the days when Artists in the modern sense had been unnecessary. Of this Frederic Mompou affords a piquant instance.

As a boy he'd attended the Conservatory of Music at Barcelona, the city where he had been born in 1893. In 1911 he escaped to Paris, like many before him, to study piano with Philipp and Lacroix, harmony with Samuel Rousseau. Although he returned to Barcelona after the statutory three

Le Jardin Retrouvé

years' studentship, French seeds were germinating in him; in 1921 he revisited Paris; and stayed there for more than twenty years. Those were the two decades of his greatest creativity. Nostalgia, however, runs deep, and Mompou was destined to return to his native Barcelona, where the latter years of his long life were as undemonstrative as his music. Since nothing 'eventful' seems to have happened to him, all that is necessary as prelude to his work is a brief commentary on the two milieux of his youth: Barcelona at the turn of the century, Paris in the twenties.

That Mompou is Catalan is crucial to his art, for a Catalan regards himself as a very special kind of Spaniard. Although Catalonia, sited at the north eastern tip of the Peninsula, cannot be divided from central and southern Spain and is historically enmeshed with Valencia, Aragon, Castile, Leon and Galicia, she is none the less closest of the Spanish nations to France. She has her own language, which mells Castilian with elements derived from old Provence; above all, she is on the Mediterranean seaboard. As Salvador de Madariaga has put it: 'a Catalan is a Spaniard who lives on the shores of the Mediterranean ... Catalonia, if not always in actual life, at least in her ideals is Greek: Greek in that classic sense which corresponds to a literary rather than to a true historical view of the Hellenic nature'. Like most Spaniards, the Catalan is a passionate individualist: prone, in the view of Castilians, to disrupt the national unity won by centuries of hard work and discipline, while exploring the European potentialities offered by his hybrid language, and by the mercantile and commercial talents fostered by his position on the eatern coast. Not surprisingly, Catalonia was in the vanguard during the revolt against Muslim rule; only much later, in the minds of nationalist extremists relatable to the lunatic fringe of Welsh and Scots nationalists in Britain today, has the Catalan cause become distinct from, even opposed to, that of Spain.

This may seem hardly pertinent to Mompou, whose tranquil spirit betrays no whiff of militancy. Even so, it may be that the association of Catalonia with progressive causes, and even with mercantile advancement, affected him powerfully, in a manner at once negative and positive: he admired and shared the Catalan's sturdy independence, while at the same time it reinforced his intuitive affinity with medieval France and therefore, by inference, his nostalgia and hermeticism. Interestingly enough, Catalan folk music embraces few erotic songs but many epic ballads and still more religious chants. The love songs tend to be pentatonic, irregular in rhythm but simple in contour, with a few chromatic or microtonally 'altered' intervals; compared with the Arabian influenced songs of the south and centre, they are not extravagantly ornamented. The epic ballads tend to be more hispanically primitive, while the religious chants betray affinities with Byzantine liturgical monody, wherein occidental and oriental traditions meet. Work songs and tambourine songs are usually diatonic major, with an occasional inflected augmented second or diminished third that hints at savagery within sturdiness. Moorish and gypsy elements intermittently erupt without seriously disturbing the music's songfulness. On the whole, Catalan folk music eschews the wilder extravagancies of southern Spain, remaining sober, even slightly austere.

The same is true of the dance music which, like most Spanish dance, is exotic, but noble in its antiquity. There is tenuous iconographical evidence that ancient Greek dance had affinities with Iberian dance, especially as practised in Catalonia. Scymnus, a rhyming geographer of the 5th century B.C., tells us that the Greeks traded wine and olives with Catalonia, and may have brought the farandole – a chain dance widespread throughout the Pyrenees – to the Iberian Peninsula; the dance's mythological origins are said to lie in the thread by means of which Theseus wound his way through the Minotaur's labyrinth! A mere three hundred years before Christ Strabo describes a circle dance which reads remarkably like a sardana: easily the most popular dance of Catalonia, which even today is based on orientally concentric rather than occidentally eccentric move-

Le Jardin Retrouvé

ment. With or without Greek antecedents, the sardana harks back to the medieval *bal rodo* or round dance which, to judge from 15th century sculptured capitals in the cloisters of Montserrat Monastery, would seem to have been an altar dance, at once secular and sacramental. Written references to the sardana first appear in the 16th century; in the 17th it was esteemed by the aristocracy, from whom it was disseminated to the people at large. By the 19th century the sardana had become pop music, the tunes being invented by composers, but often acquiring the status of folk art. Josep Ventura (1817–1875) was the father of this mini-industry which did not, in becoming slightly commercialized, sunder connections with its ancient roots. Ventura's sardana band, active in most town and village squares, modifies only slightly the traditional *cobla,* dismissing the bagpipes (delightfully known as *sac de gemecs* – sack of groans – or *la criatura verde* on account of its green baize jacket) in favour of *flavioles* (three or seven holed pipes played with one hand), of *prime* and *tenor* (clarino-like instruments of penetrating raucousness), of cornet, shawms, tambores and other tiny drums played by the flaviolist, on the analogy of pipe and tabor; flugelhorn and string bass seem to have crept in from urban sources. Although the sonority is crude and the stamping duple rhythm rude, the effect of both music and dance is, even today, light years from that of Western pop song and dance, being ceremonially dignified, non-orgiastic, a-temporal.

Performed in full, a sardana embraces a grave *introit,* a section of *curts* (short steps four bars long), followed by a section of *llargs* (long steps eight bars long). The final section, *llargs amb salts,* introduces corybantic leaps while remaining grand, even courtly. Both socially and spiritually, the sardana is stately rather than frenzied; Spanish sexuality and death-consciousness are tempered by Provençal, if not Greek, grace. Although the sardana is the quintessential Catalan dance, one finds too a few lively, even acrobatic, dances: such as the *moixiganga,* common in Sitges, and the *jota fogueada* performed, usually with fireworks, in Tarragona. Yet even these

Spain and Europe, Tradition and Mompou

vigorous dances are far from frivolity: the *moixiganga* enacts scenes from Christ's Passion, climaxing in a pyramid of male bodies figuring the Cross; the *jota fogueada* was orginally a tree-worshipping dance, grandly ritualistic if phallic.

During Mompou's childhood folk song and dance were still living realities in Catalonia, as they no longer were, of course, in industrialized Britain. He must have experienced them at first hand and foot, eye and ear; even today, when we listen to or play one of the piano pieces he calls *Cançó i dansa* we should remember that they are not mere parlour pieces, but recollections of activity that is also ritual. Although Mompou doesn't often indicate precisely which dance he is making use of, he leaves us in no doubt that the music springs from a social occasion: from carnival, Christian religious procession, or folk play that is at once a Christian resurrection myth and a pagan fertility rite. Historical and mythological dimensions coexist: *moriscas,* still widely danced in Catalonia, may record specific insurrections against Moorish oppression, while simultaneously reflecting the eternal struggle between white and black, glibly equated with good and evil. A moral bias need not be involved, only a *conjunctio oppositorum* between the rational and the irrational, between reason and instinct. We may recall that the famous Black Virgin of Montserrat is a Christian effigy said to have superseded a pagan Earth Goddess; and that while such assimilations are typical of Christianity as a whole, they are peculiarly potent in Spain, with her Moorish-African affiliations. Although this Ancient Darkness may be buried deep beneath the surface of Mompou's music, it is there.(*)

Whether Mompou was familiar with Catalan 'art' music by way of his studies at Barcelona Conservatory is more debatable.

---

* Apparently beneath the surface of the music of the sophisticated Poulenc also, for the Black Virgin is said to have boosted his perhaps fading faith. In gratitude he composed in her honour one of his most deeply affecting religious works, *Litanies à la Vierge Noire Notre-Dame de Rocamadour* (1936), scored for women's or children's voices and organ.

Le Jardin Retrouvé

He would certainly have heard the Catalan version of Roman plainchant as sung at nearby Montserrat Monastery, in those days relatively inaccessible and totally uncommercialized. Montserrat remained a musical centre throughout the Renaissance and the Baroque ages, culminating in a school of monkish composers in the 18th century. The most distinguished among them, Josep-Antoni Marti (1719–1763) and Narcia Casanoves (1747–1799) wrote, by that date, in a classical baroque idiom more Italian than Spanish, for soli, chorus, and continuo with sundry obbligato instruments. Casanoves, however, betrays evidence of the infiltration into this opulent style of a melodic austerity related both to Catalan folk song and to Montserrat plainchant, his Responses for Holy Week being at once deeply expressive and devotional. Mompou probably knew some of Casanoves's music, at least in later years after his return to Barcelona; and he must have been familiar with the work of one of the most talented, and certainly the most prolific, of Catalan composers, Padre Antonin Soler (1729–1783), some of whose string music was edited and published by Mompou's friend and colleague, Roberto Gerhard.

Today Soler is best known for his harpsichord (or fortepiano) sonatas; and rightly so, since they are by far his most exciting music. Directly modelled on those of his friend Scarlatti, they are often no less startling, and are even more darkly and authentically Spanish, as no doubt they ought to be. This is true not merely of pieces like the weird F sharp major sonata in which Soler quotes Catalan folk tunes; or which emulate savage guitar sonorities and the bray of Catalan 'orgues de Barbarie', like the lengthy but always astonishing fandango on an ostinato bass – a piece which makes most later Spanish nationalist music unnecessary. It's also true, at a deeper level, of sonatas like the D minor which Rafael Puyana, in his sleeve notes to his recording, describes as 'the most beautiful of all Soler's slow movements. I marvel at its ancient roots. While its intense quality reaches towards Beethoven and Schumann, its rhetoric is tinged with the tragic irony of the Baroque. What a strange mixture of

Spain and Europe, Tradition and Mompou

primitive and savage feelings! How many disparate tendencies unfold with ease in this most sensuous piece of music! Soler is here the child of his time at the crossroads of many past and future sources of expression'.

That defines accurately the nature of the essential Soler. None the less that was a self which, for much of his life, he tended to bury, partly because he came to accept the fashionable rococo gallantry of Italianate music, more because, having been trained at Montserrat Monastery, he spent his career as composing priest and organist of the Escorial. Much of his later music is liturgical, more easy-going and theatrical in its Italianism than is Casanoves, yet fascinatingly Hispanic if not in musical idiom, then in the way it absorbs the new into the very old. In his 12-part *Miserere* of 1766 Soler sets the verses of Psalm 50, alternating traditional plainsong intonation with his own music, scored for Italianate operatic voices and orchestra in a cross between Baroque and Classical idiom, or for monumental homophonic chorus. The work has true pathos and nobility, and its emotional neutrality is appropriate to its liturgical function. One might say the same of Mompou's one assay into orchestrally accompanied liturgical music, though this is not to suggest that he was 'influenced' by the music of this 18th century priest.

Indeed, the only local musics that may claim to irrigate the tender earth of Mompou's creation are folk song and basically medieval religious chant; and their effect on him could hardly be direct, since he was neither a Catalan peasant nor a monk, but a man or rather boy of the 20th century. He went to Paris in recognition of this, finding there not merely a different, more sophisticatedly cosmopolitan life, but also the living composers who might be relevant to him. First among them was Debussy, who of all composers of the early years of the century most heralded a new dawn, and was therefore pertinent to a composer of *renouvellement*. As we'll see, Mompou's music seldom sounds 'like' Debussy's; but he found much that he needed in the revolutionary aspects of Debussy's technique: his static harmony, his decoratively incremental, non-developing line, his use of timbre ('colour') in association with immobile drones and rotatory ostinati, even the aesthetic whereby Debussy, in answer to a bemused academic, announced that the only 'rule' he followed was 'mon plaisir'. Debussy's 'moments of sensation' were often associated with childhood. In Spain he found a dream-world he did not need to visit, since the primitive modality, rhythmic irregularity and non-harmonic organum techniques of Spanish traditional musics awoke in him immediate echoes. According to Manuel de Falla, who should know, piano pieces of Debussy like *La Soirée dans Grenade* and *La Puerta del Vino*, and even more the orchestral *Iberia*, are 'in the smallest detail redolent of Spain'.

In Paris Mompou also met Ravel, and found in his work, as did everyone, many of the qualities that distinguish Debussy. He found something else too: the characteristic Ravel *tune*, 'antique', modal, Medieval, Renaissance, Baroque. There is a Ravel tune as there is not a Debussy tune, and Mompou's melodies belong to the same category, though they are not imitative. That there should be consanguinity is not surprising, for Ravel's modal melodies are often associated with childhood and the fairy-tale, as in *La Mere d'Oye*, based on Perrault's elegantly seventeenth century retelling of the old stories. One of the most beautiful of such tunes is given to the Princess in *L'Enfant et les Sortilèges*, specifically a parable about childhood and the Fall. Another late piece, *Chansons Madécasses*, relates the Arab-African savages' 'green paradise of childish loves' to Eden; the 'innocent' Negro is transported to Parisian cabaret in the blues of the (also late) Violin Sonata, while gypsy outlaws insinuate themselves into an expensive Parisian restaurant in the *Tzigane*, also for violin and piano.

All these childhood evocations betray a Spanish or Moorish tinge, not surprisingly since for Ravel even more than for Debussy Spain was a home from home. He was born in the Basque country only a few miles from the Spanish border, and

Spain and Europe, Tradition and Mompou

as a child heard Spanish folk songs sung by his parents, who had lived over the Pyrenees for prolonged periods. His physical appearance was more than a little Iberian; his first fully personal composition, the *Habanera* of 1895, is overtly Spanish, as are the *Rapsodie Espagnole* and *L'Heure Espagnole,* not to mention the ubiquitous *Bolero.* That Ravel's Spanishness plumbs deeper than local colour is revealed in the *Pavane pour une Infante Défunte,* the insidious tune of which relates the Hispanic theme to the antique modality of the *conte de fées:* as does the sadly serene slow movement of the two-handed Piano Concerto, of which the first movement too is seductively Iberian beneath its Parisian chic. The darker, deeper, more alien aspects of Spain reverberate through the Concerto for piano left hand. Can it have been the (physically) *sinister* nature of this piece that intuitively prompted Ravel to reveal through it such (metaphysically) black magic – which indeed emerges from the near-total *darkness* of doublebasses and double bassoon? One of Ravel's last works concerns Don Quixote.

The third Parisian composer in whom Mompou recognized a kindred spirit was Erik Satie: a musical poet of childhood who has qualities in common with Debussy and Ravel, while differing profoundly from them. Mompou is often likened to Satie for the superficial reasons that both composers use few notes and often dispense with bar-lines. But although there is a genuine affinity between Mompou's music and Satie's non-developing pattern-making and non-functional harmony, alike in his early Rosicrucian period and in his café-concert and geometrically neo-classic phases, the similarity is *only* superficial. There may even be more kinship between Mompou and his younger contemporary Francis Poulenc, in early youth a disciple of Satie, and always a guardian of the heritage of French civilization from the Middle Ages to the 19th century, and a hedonistic bard of *la Belle France* and *les charmes de la vie.* This again is more a matter of spiritual brotherhood than of influence: as is still more the case with any kinship between

Le Jardin Retrouvé

Mompou and the popular Provençal aspects of Milhaud, whose native habitat, on the other side of the Pyrenees, was not far distant from Mompou country.

Mompou has little in common with his Spanish contemporaries, though any Catalan composer of his generation must owe a debt to Felipe Pedrell (1841–1922), not so much for his creative work as for his labours towards the rehabilitation of Spanish music, both in its folk and in its artistic traditions. At this date it doesn't greatly matter that Pedrell aimed to do for Spanish what Wagner did for German opera; it does matter that, but for his efforts in collecting and notating folk songs and in editing and publishing the 'early' Hispanic masters, it would have been difficult for a young Spanish composer even to know what his heritage was. Despite his presumptive Wagnerism, Pedrell was the first Spanish composer to absorb 'old' Spanish music into his own work, notably in his opera *La Celestina* (1904), which gave him a hint in being based on a classic 15th century love story. Henceforth the process of assimilation could be spontaneous, as it is in Falla and, modestly, in Mompou.

Significantly, there is some link between Mompou and the most potent Spanish composer nurtured in the 19th century, Isaac Albéniz: or at least with his one great work, *Iberia,* the large-scale sequence of piano pieces he finished, in Paris, in 1909. That was just before Mompou went there, but he would certainly have heard the dazzling music played by Ricardo Viñes, the Spanish pianist living in Paris, who did so much for the cause of the new Parisian composers. That Mompou's discreet music should have common ground with Albéniz's *Iberia,* which often evokes the dark wildness of ancient Spain, is surprising though not, as we'll see, fortuitous.

There is also a kinship between Mompou and the 'archaic', medieval-Renaissance, Don Quixotic Falla of *Master Peter's Puppet Show* (1924) and of the Harpsichord Concerto (1923), though those marvellous pieces postdate Mompou's formative works. Remembering that Gertrude Stein remarked that if you scratch a Spaniard you find a Saracen or Tartar, it is pertinent to

Spain and Europe, Tradition and Mompou

note that Stravinsky was also living in Paris along with Mompou. The Spanish street-and-church music of Falla's puppet opera and harpsichord concerto is not far from Stravinsky's peasant church and fairground, though there's not much in common between Stravinsky and Mompou except for the patterned ostinati. Albéniz's *Iberia* portrays wide regions of Spain while evading Catalonia; Falla's muse is Castilian rather than northern. In any case, comparisons can serve only to fit Mompou into context. He was a composer as a child, before he went to Paris. Arrived there, he already had a 'voice' and, in a sense, all the technique he needed. No composer deeply affected his identity, though Debussy, Ravel, Satie, and possibly Albéniz, helped him to discover what that identity was. This is the process we will trace in examining his apprentice-work, *Impresiones Intimas*, composed between 1911 and 1914, when European War threatened everyone's childhood.

II

Mompou's Apprenticeship: a Path through the Garden

> Childhood, childhood, where have you gone?
> Will you come back to us?
> Will you come back?
> Ever come back?
>
> SAPPHO: *translated Peter Whigham*

> groping
> beneath
> the sleep
> of ocean,
> searching the sea-bed
> for the
> pearl self-
> formed in
> boyhood
>
> THE VIth DALAI LAMA:
> *translated Peter Whigham*

SINCE the small piano pieces that make up Mompou's *Impresiones Intimas* were written at various times between the ages of sixteen and twenty-one, they are unlikely to have been planned as a set. None the less they cohere, adumbrating most of the modes and manners the young composer is to explore during his first creative phase. They are remarkably assured, coming from so young a man; indeed one might say that they reveal, as do Chopin's near-incredible opus 10 *Études*, a personality already formed which, during the passage of years, the composer will refine but hardly improve upon.

The cycle opens with three little pieces each one page long, originally entitled, in Catalan, *Planys* (plaint). In the published

Mompou's Apprenticeship: a Path through the Garden

version Mompou dropped the title, though it defines the nature of the music, suggesting both a medieval religious lament and the 'complaint' of a troubadour lover to his lady. No. 1, *Lento molto espressivo*, has irregular and infrequent bar-lines indicative of phrase structure rather than of temporal progression. It is in the aeolian mode on A or transposed to E; is in four quasi-vocal parts more or less within singing compass; and consists of two five-beat phrases, the second of which is a slightly modified repeat of the first; with a coda consisting of two four-beat phrases rounded off by a two-bar cadence. For the most part the texture is 'white note' modality, the melody floating up through an A minor triad and gently declining on to a chord intensified by the first appearance of a chromatic note, G sharp. Passing dissonances of seventh and ninth creep in, as they do in the white note writing of Ravel or for that matter Stravinsky and Satie. That the music already sounds like no composer other than Mompou must be due to the Catalan-folk or Provençal-troubadour lyricism of the melody or melodies (for each of the four lines is singable). The equilibrium between melodic 'innocence' and harmonic 'experience' is manifest in the fact that the chromaticized G produces within the polyphony a harmonic, which becomes a tonal, intensification: the bass leaps a tritone from C to F sharp, initiating a modulation, by way of a tender dominant thirteenth, into aeolian E minor, with a quasi-sixteenth century ornamental resolution. In the repeat the upper arch is extended a tone higher to B instead of A, and the chromaticized chord on the descent is more emotive in being a *triple* suspension. The coda-like statement of the arch rises to the original A again, but refers obliquely to the B, written echo-style in small notation, in the declining phrase:

Le Jardin Retrouvé

The consummatory final bars, all a descent, add extra parts to produce a denser texture, and incorporate both the G sharp and F sharp into the final cadence.

The second Plaint is also in the aeolian mode on A, but in a gently swaying pulse in 3 4; the phrases are of five-bar duration. Basically, the texture is again in four quasi-vocal parts, though the lines here move note for note, in Renaissance discantus style. The 'antique' flavour – recalling medieval-Renaissance Poulenc as much as Ravel – is reinforced by low-tolling bells on A or E. The significance of bells in Mompou's music will be discussed in the next chapter; here it suffices to say that the bell-pedals combine with the undulating white-note seventh chords to create harmonic stasis only momentarily broken by two chromatic notes, F sharp and D sharp, in the five-bar cadential phrase. The repeat of the clause resolves by way of a dominant minor ninth, sounding more than normally pathetic in this harmonically sober context. That the da capo is unaltered enhances the piece's wistfulness; its tranquil melancholy, like Time itself, goes on.

Such is the mood of the third Plaint also, for which Mompou shifts the mode up a semitone to aeolian B flat. The music now flows *gracioso* in 6/8, a four-bar phrase being answered by one of five bars. The little tune or melody* is more folk-like than liturgical in flavour; it suggests a child's rune* – another Mompou motif to be discussed in a later chapter. Melodically, it could hardly be simpler: a scale rises through a fourth from tonic B flat to E flat, marked *tenuto*; is twice repeated; then falls

---

* In this book, without attempting to be rigidly systematic, I use the words 'gesture', 'cry', 'chant' to indicate the most fundamental type of melodic utterance, derivable from the pathological yell of instinctual feeling. 'Rune' and 'tune' I use for the primitive types of melodic pattern imposed on the yell – patterns which are usually symmetrical and repetitive, as in tribal dances and the singing games of children. 'Melody' I use in reference to higher types of linear organization, which may but need not be repetitive, and will be prone to extension and evolution in Time. 'Melodies' in this sense may or may not also involve a harmonic dimension.

Mompou's Apprenticeship: a Path through the Garden

of its own weight. The bass oscillates between G flat and F, while the left hand figuration hints at a little countermelody within a spread arpeggio; in the fourth bar a cadential A natural momentarily disturbs the modality:

The answering clause begins a third higher, fills in the rising scale with richer triadic chords, but fades on the modal flat seventh undulating to the tonic. The rest of the piece telescopes the cadential phrase with the first bar of the tune, repeats bars 2 to 6 unchanged, and adds an unambiguously modal two-bar code. The piece is a mini-miracle. One cannot explain how such minimal material – a four note rising scale many times repeated – produces so moving a sense of vernal promise, of young life – and love? – opening in the dawn. If a 'plaint', this is also – to maintain the medieval-Renaissance terminology – an alba or aubade.

The fourth of the *Impresiones Intimas* is exceptional in the cycle in that it is the only piece that moves fast (*agitato*), and even grows loud. Less child-like, more adolescent, than the plaints, it hints at another of Mompou's loves, Chopin, whose significance in relation to the Catalan composer will be discussed in a later chapter. Like a Chopin *Etude*, this piece adheres throughout to a consistent figuration: broken chords in syncopation, over a 'walking' bass in quavers. The modality may be phrygian on A, with sharpened sixth, though one hears

Le Jardin Retrouvé

the music harmonically and rhythmically rather than linearly. A one-bar 4/4 phrase is played twice, with a sharply chromaticized final beat, the two bars being then repeated a fifth higher. Another two bars, moving in sequential ninths, balance the previous four. The tempo changes from 4 to 3/4, and a balancing section over a dominant, which changes to a tonic, pedal dissolves in syncopated chromatics. The effect is, for Mompou, fervent; yet the Spanish gypsyish passion of the fluttering syncopations and undulating chromatics is, as with Chopin, stabilized by the sequences and sustained pedal notes. For two bars, after the 3/4 section, the gentle tumult ceases in favour of dotted minim whole-tone chords, asking questions. Both the 4/4 and the 3/4 sections are then repeated, and rounded off with a coda in which the chromatics flicker through a tonic pedal to resolve resonantly in A major. The undulating flow suggests a water image such as one finds frequently in Chopin and other romantic piano music: water being an image of dream and of the unconscious life. Maybe this is the youthful Mompou in Paris, breasting troubled waters by virtue of spiritual simplicity and with the help of those anchoring pedal notes! The piece also reminds us of another familiar Chopin image – that of a caged bird longing to soar, beating its wings against a prison, perhaps of the past. The D major Prelude from opus 28 is a small instance among many more elaborate ones in the *Etudes*.

Mompou's next 'impression', *Pájaro triste, is* a caged bird, though he's not beating his wings against anything but is sadly passive in his imprisonment. The piece is said to be based on the cry of a pet linnet, a pre-conscious avian creature who utters a motif of falling minor third, sometimes extended to a fourth. Such declensions are typical of primitive lament everywhere, from birds and beasts to children and savages. Each cry swings in a slow triple pulse, in a pentatonic-aeolian C sharp; and resolves in sighing double suspensions over a drone on tonic and fifth:

Mompou's Apprenticeship: a Path through the Garden

There is no real modulation, though the second two-bar clause shifts momentarily to mixolydian E. This six-bar clause is answered by one of five bars, inverting and filling in the melodic thirds, now accompanied by parallel secundal chords in E major. Both clauses are repeated, the 'echoes' being extended into a coda. The humanly expressive dissonances are intensifications of the linnet's plaintive peep, imbuing the 'young' sensibility with the bird's vulnerability. Despite its primitivism, this is a very artful little piece, its oddly moving effect dependent on its rudimentariness.

La barca is even more mysterious: another water image, yet distinct from the water images of Chopin, Liszt, Debussy and Ravel. The bass at first consists merely of dropping minor thirds C flat to A flat – the same 'pre-conscious' cry uttered by the linnet and by children everywhere. Above this bass Mompou writes three real parts in middle register. The melody in the top line rises through a tritone, asking an unanswered question; the alto and tenor dissonantly undulate, grinding with one another against the bass, like oars in the *barca's* rowlock. The upward rising phrase is answered by a free inversion, with false relations between the melodic B flat and an *upward*-pushing B natural, which is not identical with the bass's C flat. Tender aspiration subsides in a four-bar coda of sequential sevenths. It seems as though the eleven-bar clause is to be repeated, still more tranced and entrancing in its watery undulations; but at the coda phrase the music modulates from the lulling A flat major to a dominant seventh on F minor and thence to a wide-spaced dominant ninth of B flat minor: which disperses in a German sixth F flat to D natural, echoing into silence:

Le Jardin Retrouvé

A tiny, but poignant, harmonic climax is thus effected, before the music fades into the original questioning phrase, with its lulling-lapping accompaniment, the base still drooping in its minor third, the inner parts softly grinding until they're stilled – or nearly stilled, since the rhythm is syncopated – on an A flat major triad.

The next piece, *Cuna,* is pitched a semitone higher, on A, and if less mysterious than *La barca,* is related to it since it is a lullaby in a slow-lilting 12/8, its rhythm that of a watery barcarolle. The accompanying figure rocks between a low tonic crotchet and caressing semiquavers on the dominant E and B. The tune begins as a simple pentatonic declension, repeated with the intrusion of a sharp lydian fourth; chromaticized broken chords fill in the middle register. The answering phrase begins on a Debussyan dominant ninth of C, flows expansively into a melodic falling sixth; the climax, when the phrase is repeated, is of almost Ravellian opulence, resolving back from a chromaticized C minor to A major, with tremulous 'added' notes. The piece is then repeated da capo, with the sequential dominant ninths – Debussyan echoes soon to become uncharacteristic of Mompou – considerably amplified before their German sixth resolution. The added notes at the end are radiant, over the rocking bass. This piece is another child's rune, though those dominant ninth chords are 'conscious' enough – even a shade *self*-conscious.

Mompou's Apprenticeship: a Path through the Garden

The title of the penultimate piece, *Secreto,* defines its nature. This very hermetic little piece takes us to the heart of Mompou's magic, and is the first number in the cycle to make overt reference to Catalan folk music, though the tune is his own. The 'secret' quality is enhanced by the fact that it is notated in seven sharps, in C sharp major, though the sevenths are usually flattened, in mixolydian modality. The melody flows gently up the scale in dotted rhythm, breaks off, subsides through falling fourth and third, cadences through the flat seventh. The left hand's accompaniment, widely spaced, sways through the dotted rhythm; despite the thin scoring, its spacing produces a rich harmonic texture, with seventh and ninth chords implied rather than stated. The mordents and flamenco-flavoured decoration in the answering clause sound archaic, and the harmonic suspensions are tinged with regret; the melancholy of the forlornly floating tune suggests *lacrimae rerum,* in the context of the harmonic sensitivity of the solitary heart, sensuous but child-like, hugging its secret, in all those heavenly sharps!:

After the melody's second clause the rocking rhythm ceases for a two-bar cadence on to a G sharp minor triad – a flattened dominant. The rest of the piece repeats twice what we've already heard, but resolves the cadence phrase into a G sharp *major* triad, dissipating over a solemn bell of low C sharps. The

Le Jardin Retrouvé

piece is dedicated to Josefina Miró. If she is a relation of the painter, that would be appropriate, for Miró is indeed a painter of childhood's 'secreto'.

The final piece in the cycle, *Gitanos*, extending to five pages, is easily the longest, though this does not mean that Mompou is creating more structurally developed music, since the form is a rondo or round dance. Repetition rather than development is the principle, for after each 'episode' the tune is restated, unchanged. Rondo is, of course, one of the techniques whereby folk music *goes on,* as long as is functionally necessary for working, dancing or miming to. In this case the dancers are gypsies, this being Mompou's first patent reference to these outcasts from society who are another basic motif in his work. Like all Mompou's gypsies, these are *inquieto,* dancing in a syncopated triple measure to a mixolydian tune that might be a street game. When the four-bar clause is answered by one of five bars the folk modality is momentarily banished by a sharp seventh, taking us to diatonic G major. Sequential thirteenth and ninth chords create a sensuous harmonic perturbation to balance the rhythmic excitation. Though this is a more conventional piece than the magical *La barca* and *Secreto* it effectively follows the behests of the gypsies' secret (child-like?) hearts, the music's inquietude being at once age-old and Mompou's own, youthfully, in Paris. With each repetition the episodes introduce harsher percussive appoggiaturas over the unchanging syncopated pedals; they could be extended ad infinitum, or at least until the dancers are tired, as would happen if real gypsies were dancing in the present moments. Mompou's piano piece, however, ends with a fadeout which negates Time. Jazz pianists do the same, for similar reasons. Looking back on the cycle in retrospect, one may detect traces of jazz pianism in, for instance, the 'climax', if the word is permissible, to *La barca,* in which the refined chromatics almost suggest Bill Evans. This is of course an affinity, not an influence – Mompou's piece predates Evans by more than forty years. The general implications of the affinity between some aspects of Mompou's piano

Mompou's Apprenticeship: a Path through the Garden

idiom and 'white' jazz pianism will be discussed in a later chapter.

In *Impresiones Intimas* Mompou adolescently explores the modes and manners he is to investigate in later years, from cry, gesture and incantation to child's rune and tune, to folk song and dance, to aspects of European art music, mostly 'old' monody and polyphony, and early Romantic pianism. After this prospective survey he turns to rudiments, abandoning, for the 'time being', much of historical Europe. His next few works explore what might almost be called *pre*-history, concentrating on 'moments' without before and after, as manifest in primitive charms and spells. In so doing he offers an extreme instance of the 20th century's sophisticated consciousness of unconsciousness.

III

Mompou, Bells and Spells

Had everybody such chimes, foes would be turned into friends and everyone would live in the most beautiful harmony.

Papageno, of his bells, in Mozart's *Magic Flute*.

Magic is a representation where the emotion evoked is an emotion valued on account of its function in practical life, evoked in order that it may discharge that function, and fed by the generative or focusing magical life into the practical life that needs it. Magical activity is a kind of dynamo supplying the mechanism of the practical life with the emotional current that drives it. Hence magic is a necessity for every sort and condition of man, and is actually found in every healthy society. A society which thinks, as our own thinks, that it has outlived the need for magic is either mistaken in that opinion, or else it is a dying society, perishing for lack of interest in its own maintenance.

L. G. COLLINGWOOD: *The Principles of Art*

THE musical synonym for 'pre-consciousness' is the bell.* Both real bells (inverted cups, usually of metal, hit with an attached clapper or externally activated hammer) and crotals (hollowed gourd-like objects with a free body, such as pea or pebble, inserted) may be said to belong to God in that they *reveal* the acoustical properties of Nature. Some 26,000 years before

---

* This discussion of the philosophy and psychology of campanology incorporates material from my Times Literary Supplement review of Percival Price's book *Bells and Man*: to which it is therefore indebted.

Mompou, Bells and Spells

Christ the Chinese Emperor Chuan Hao 'struck the bell and called the attention of the people, so that he could teach them righteousness'; the teaching came *after* the submission to Nature. Chinese bells were decorated with dragons and other fabulous creatures lest demons should threaten the transcendental power whereby bells sustained the Universal Harmony; without truly resonating bells the universe might collapse. Most ancient oriental cultures regarded bells as agents and activators of magic. Hindus found in them the circle, hemisphere and lotus basic to their cosmology, and saw in the relation of drum to bell the immemorial symbolism of sword and chalice. In Burma, Asia and Japan bell and drum were likewise aural incarnations of yin and yang, while flower-like crotals represented atropaic forces. With all these peoples the consecrated bell 'affects gods and informs mortals', with results normally benevolent but occasionally malevolent, according to who strikes the resonator, how and when. And although in African and Latin American cultures bells tend to be less hieratically solemn, they usually function in a religious context.

Even in the old oriental cultures, however, the power of bells has declined over the centuries. Little Japanese girls still dance with the suzuki or 'crotal tree' as waistband, adding its aural tingle to their visually glittering garments, but they would be surprised to learn that the purpose of the crotal tree is to lure the sun goddess Amaterasu from the Cave of Heaven. Similarly, bells which in ancient Hindu and Chinese cultures were employed as agents for converse with the gods now summon minions to the desks of government officials, or instigate exeunts at closing time in libraries, museums, and even pubs. Not that the sacred import of bells obviated, even in old cultures, more practical uses. In India bells attached to cows not only paid tribute to a sacred animal; they also helped to locate its presence, and there was economic as well as religious advantage in the fact that the better beast had the better bell. Muslims were singular in allowing bells to be used *only* for practical ends; as religious objects they were suspect since their

Le Jardin Retrouvé

reverberations cluttered air-space better devoted to prayer. This suspicion spilled over into Christian Europe, St. Paul dismissing bells along with the sounding cymbal as illusory appurtenances of the heathen.

By about A.D. 400, however, bells had been introduced, reputedly at the instigation of St. Paulinus of Nola, as a call to Christian worship and as protection against demonic forces. Christ's scriptural 'knocking at the door' was analogized in three stages: the wooden *sematron*, representing the Old Testament prophets, the clanking entrance bell, representing the New Testament Gospels, and the monastery bell itself as the trumpet of the Lord. From the 11th century onwards Christian bells rapidly proliferated from monastery to parish church, where they came to serve civic as well as ecclesiastical functions. Curfew and angelus had social significance in controlling behaviour in the community, as well as spiritual significance in (negatively) counteracting things that go bump in the night, and in (positively) paying homage to the Virgin Mary. Bells now indicated not only the progress of the liturgy and of the church year but also the diurnal cycle of town and village activities. Soon bells erected in ecclesiastical buildings had rival owners in church and state, and fulfilled interrelated social, political and military as well as religious purposes. This multiplicity of function was expanded when religious buildings were complemented by civic guildhalls, the bells of which regulated the commercial calendar. It is difficult to imagine the campanological hullabaloo within which medieval and early Renaissance folk lived. Large and middle-sized bells informed and instructed them in a vast diversity of divine and civic functions from the rising of the sun to its setting; tiny bells attached to the clothing of priests, courtiers, jesters and even common people, not to mention cattle, sheep and goats, provided an incessant aural halo to their human and beastly occupations, from the most hallowed to the most mundane.

The beginning of the end of the bell-cosmos occurs when, as the Renaissance prospers, bells become explicit chronometers, measuring time essential for commercial intercourse, rather than affirming its triviality in the eye and ear of God. During the 17th and 18th centuries increasingly elaborate mechanical contraptions – artificial men who register Time by a clockwork hammering – denature and demagic bells to make them play *our* music rather than their own, or God's. Originally most bells had at least sought affinity with those wind-bells that produce natural partials in response to the air's God-directed buffet or caress. At the onset of the scientific revolution mathematician-philosophers like Mersenne and Descartes offer blueprints for the acoustical properties of carillons, demonstrating how man could intellectually control their forging and ultimately their mass-manufacture. The process ends with the bells that tinkle 'Rudolf the Red-nose Reindeer' in our Christmastide emporia, and in the chiming competitions organized by American churches not for the glory of God, nor even to remind men of social and agricultural obligations, but in rivalry with other churches: the cleverest chimes, by our fallible human standards, attract the most customers and therefore the most fairly filthy lucre – and so, one presumes, please our greedy god the most.

Bells were already losing their magic powers in the 18th century, by which time few 'art' composers – as distinct from those Medieval and Renaissance musicians still involved with bells in liturgical and civic contexts – made reference to them. True, Bach still called on bells, with defined theological connotations, nuptial or funerary. But he was an old-fashioned composer, and by the end of the century Enlightened men had little artistic truck with these magical instruments. Mozart's Papageno is the exception that proves the rule, since he and his bells were an implicit criticism of 18th century Rationality. Less directly, the same is true of the celestial bell-sounds which Beethoven, in his last three piano sonatas, emulated by way of multiple trills that disperse 'Western' harmonic consciousness. Romantic composers such as Berlioz, Liszt, Verdi and Wagner exploit the supernatural effect of bells dramatically, even melodramatically, in the context of materialistic societies. But if

Le Jardin Retrouvé

one concentrates on the ritualistic rather than artistic significance of bells one has to admit that their story, chronologically considered, reflects little credit on the human race. Passing-bell and death-knell, which had imbued medieval people with the terror of mortality but also with a sense of human achievement, have for us been trivialized; even our carillons of jubilation, celebrating the illusory victories of our death-dealing war-machines, come across as a 'resounding tinkle'. But we shouldn't be too hard on ourselves. The sexton who in a remote (but 20th century) village prided himself on having, through his expert bell-ringing, diverted a tempest from his own to a neighbour village must have had precedents for such unChristian behaviour. Ungenerosity of spirit is not peculiar to ages of unfaith.

During the late nineteenth and early twentieth centuries bells maintained their pristine magic only in relatively primitive social orders that had to a degree bypassed the European Renaissance: as is manifest in, for instance, the terrifying clock scene in Mussorgsky's *Boris Godunov, passim* throughout his *Pictures at an Exhibition,* and in many scenes from Janáček's operas and in the prelude and postlude to his *Sinfonietta*. And it was by way of such primitivists that bells inveigled their way into the magic heart of twentieth century music, especially that of the centrally regressive-progressive Debussy. That bell sounds and the piano's natural overtones are in accord with Debussy's static notion of harmony is obvious; and in this respect Scriabin, Messiaen, Varèse, Cage and West-coast orientalists like Lou Harrison and Alan Hovhaness are Debussy's heirs, as are 'advanced' pop groups like Tubular Bells and Tangerine Dream. Relevant to this is the often quoted fact that Debussy was thrilled by the Javanese gamelan music he heard at the Paris Exhibition. Most of the composers mentioned in the previous sentence have incorporated elements from Javanese, Balinese and Polyesian musics into their Western-based art; Lou Harrison, Harry Partch and Steve Reich have made justly-intoned bell sonorities the basis of a musical

Mompou, Bells and Spells

philosophy consciously reviving the unconscious 'cosmology' of bells referred to at the beginning of this chapter.

This being so, we will not be surprised that Mompou, self-styled composer of *recommencement* and *renouvellement*, should, even more than Debussy, have heard in bells the genesis of his re-creation. Although for the adolescent Mompou to have been consciously aware of what he was doing would have been a contradiction in terms, he seems to have known intuitively that bell-cosmology implied a new-old approach to the rudiments of music. In particular, it meant that a composer must recognize that the terms *sound, tone* and *note* have specific meanings, much confused in modern usage. As the composer-astrologist Dane Rudhyar has pointed out, a *sound* simply refers to the transmission of vibrations in the air, and their perception by the auditory centre of the human brain. A *tone* is a sound that 'has conveyed (or can convey) significant information to the consciousness of the hearer because it is charged with and transmits (or can transmit) the special nature and character of the source of the sound. Thus a *tone* is a meaning-carrying sound ... A musical *note*, on the other hand, has no meaning in itself. It has meaning only in relation to other notes'. Mompou invites us to listen first to sounds as they are (bell-like) 'in themselves'; then to tones and to intervals, which define the relationship of one tone to another, in order to effect transmission of the magical will. 'Primitive' peoples did and do this in their sacred rituals wherein they participate in the creative powers of the gods. We no longer have such rituals; but we *may* still discover magic in the quality of tones and in their ability to communicate meaning. This is what happens when we allow ourselves to enter the circle of Mompou's *Cants Magics:* the first of a series of works – almost apotheoses of the bell – which carry Debussy's liberation of harmony from line, of sound from antecedence and consequence, to a *ne plus ultra*. In *Cants Magics,* composed in 1917 (the first of the West-destroying wars was still raging), Mompou becomes a young shaman to a hyper-civilized, but decadent, tribe.

Le Jardin Retrouvé

The first *cant* — incantation rather than song — has a first section consisting of one unchanging chord, spread across the keyboard, swinging like a tolling bell or censer. Above an empty fifth in bass register, an E minor triad is appended, with added major sixth, ringing into space and distance. Beginning *energic*, the pulse gradually slows down through its triple metre, like a pendulum swinging to rest. A duple-rhythmed middle section, *lent*, doesn't relinquish the low fifth, but the added sixth chord above it is more richly spaced and, oscillating up and down a tone, generates a rune-like tune in two-bar periods. With no hint of harmonic development, the section fades into pedalled resonance. The *energic* triple-beat swaying returns, on the same chord, for four unbarred measures, but then with the C sharp flattened to C natural. The contracted dissonance scrunches, but doesn't sound like an expressive appoggiatura, because it isn't. It is simply a sonority, built on 'primitive' fourths, inducing a nervous frisson but going, and seeking to go, nowhere:

The second *cant* does have a rudimentary theme, or at least rune or tune, as well as a tone and interval. A two-bar pentatonic phrase is four times repeated, hypnotically, in base register. This is marked *obscur;* but the sonority clears when the rune-tune appears in the treble, accompanied by broken or unbroken forms of a B minor triad, sometimes with added second. The cadence moves up the scale from the B minor chord to G, also with added second as bass. After a double bar, tempo doubles. The tune, still unchanged, appears in middle register; the harmony-notes teeter again between B and G, with scrunchily dissonant added seconds. High up is a filigree of scintillating bells, alternating perfect and imperfect fourths, *brillant* in

Mompou, Bells and Spells

small notation. Briefly, modality shifts up a tone to D flat standing for C sharp, and the metre expands from 2/2 to 3/2. The treble bells change almost imperceptibly back to quivery fourths and fifths of pentatonic B minor, floating into silence. Through this the rune-tune re-emerges, unchanged, unchanging. A *molt lent* coda sounds quintessentially Mompou-like, though it merely moves through that B minor triad with added second, a tenth F sharp to A with added seventh, and a final empty fifth, echoing to stillness:

The bells in the fourth *cant* are those of a funeral procession: which simply celebrates the irremediable fact of death, without any of the salutations to humanity's potential if inevitably defeated heroism that typify the funeral marches of a Beethoven or Mahler. A powerful sonority is generated from very few notes, as the melodic pattern – there is here hardly a tune – alternates in metrical regularity between minor and major second, above the tolling of a cavernous E flat pedal note. This booming bell deepens to low B flat when the incantatory two-bar motif is repeated, its swaying seconds decorated with ephemeral chromatics. Mompou tells us to play *sous le poid du sommeil*, release into bell-nature being also release into sleep's unconsciousness, though the static chords are acid, as compared with Debussy's soft cocoon of sound. Another repeat adds arpeggiated quivers (*una mica d'aire*) around the rune and the bells, but the low B flat persists until the music returns to its starting point. In the final clause the triads, slowly swaying in contrary motion over the unmoving E flat pedal, disturb by their harmonic inconsequentiality, and by the end even the pedal itself is ambiguous. The C minor triad above the low E flat doesn't sound like 'added sixth' harmony, though the pedal

Le Jardin Retrouvé

note makes the triad irresolute, resounding into silence — once more bell-like.

The fourth *cant*, marked *misterios*, opens in pentatonic C minor, carrying on from the previous piece: from which it evolves a quasi-medieval, folk-flavoured 'gesture' accompanied by tambour-like reiterations of a low C, replacing the ambiguous E flat. A symmetrical four-bar phrase is repeated, but then swept away by a rapid, relatively loud section marked *sans ordre*. The disorderliness springs from the left hand's turbulently arpeggiated figuration; but turbulence doesn't imply harmonic movement since the rapid figuration is an ostinato pattern that incorporates added seconds into a C minor triad. The right hand unfolds a figuration that is a more melodic inversion of the left hand, but also an extension of the original, quasi-medieval tune:

The section peters out in fourths: to be followed by a *tranquil-triste* passage which veils the original tune in G flat bell-triads. The tonality equivocates between C minor and E flat minor until, in another repeat, the tune, still at original pitch, is harmonized in glowing G flat major arpeggios, petering out in whole-tone oscillations. A da capo of the *viù* section dissolves (*doloros*) into 'primitive' falling fourths and an unresolved D above the spread C minor triad.

There are a magical five of these magic chants, the last of which, restricted to tone and interval, is the most patently bell-based. In the first section what counts for theme is simply a spread arpeggio of F major, in calmly measured duple pulse. Chromatic chords add upper partials between each tolling of the triadic motif; usually the overtone chords, printed in small notes, have bitonal implications with the triad, though they are

Mompou, Bells and Spells

not 'grammatically' dissonant appoggiaturas. At the end of the bell-tolling the triad changes momently from major to minor, and the *calma* first section leads into a swaying 6/8, marked *inquiet*. One suspects an instrusion of Mompou's anxious gypsies here; the tune's oscillations between whole and half tone cadence in a plaintive descent through a diminished fourth, while the accompanying figure rocks between D flat and A flat. The first section is repeated undisturbed by gypsy inquietude, the bell-tone doubled at the upper octave. In the coda the added sixth over the resounding but quiet low F is alchemized from major to minor, only to return to major with wide-spaced added second, sixth and ninth. The sonority glows, almost palpitates, intimating bells' therapeutic potential. One couldn't hope for a more telling instance of the distinction between tones and notes.

But if Mompou's *cants magics* function mainly through tones and intervals, we have noted how *modes* embryonically evolved within them. As Dane Rudhyar again pointed out, the shaman chanted as birds sing or cats caterwaul; he had learned, and remembered, the traditional way to achieve magical results. When, at a slightly more advanced stage of consciousness, primitive man began to sing he unconsciously organized the relationships *between* tones in accord with acoustic principles. A mode is such a functional arrangement of tones; and the Sanskrit word for it, *grama*, originally meant a village, in which each man, woman and child, like each tone, had specific significance. The *grama* was a 'whole of vibratory energies, just as the village was a whole of homes and families.' The modes of medieval and Renaissance Europe preserve much of this holy and holistic significance, at least as compared with the equal tempered *scales* of the modern world, and we'll see how Mompou's later music relates, in this respect, to Christian tradition. Back in 1920, however, he was concerned rather with the ways in which mode *germinates:* as is evident in another set of small piano pieces in the shape of non-developing spells or incantations. He called them *Charmes,* and again allowed them to spring, as it were of their own volition, from the properties of

Le Jardin Retrouvé

tones. At the same time their infantilism, using the word in no discreditable sense, has specific human motivations: tones and intervals lead to gestures, creating mode, and acquiring therapeutic properties. Having defined a charm as a *forme primitive d'incantation*, Mompou tells us, in French, what these properties are, in respect of each piece. The music is far more primitive melodically, rhythmically and harmonically than Debussy, and betrays virtually no influence of recognized art composers nor of folk music except in so far as many of the linear and rhythmic formulae, being so rudimentary, must occur in any instinctive musical language. Yet the pieces are 'realized' with impeccable precision; the charm (in the colloquial sense) of these charms (in the anthropological sense) springs, perhaps, from this paradox.

The function of the first charm is *pour endormir la souffrance* and, working by hypnosis, it does. Through a metrically regular triple pulse the left hand softly plays quavers rocking between the tritone A to E flat and the G below the A. The right hand noodles a little rune-tune, with filigreed decoration, around the tones F and C, the tonality being mixolydian on F. This tritone – like those in early Messiaen which of course it predates – is tonally neutral rather than devilish in the medieval sense. An inner part, drooping down the scale, emulates little bells. When in the tune's fourth bar the ostinato shifts down a tone to an A flat bass and then to F sharp (equals G flat), there's a piquant false relation between the harmony notes and the A flat and F natural of the melody;

The first clause ends with the ostinato slipping a further semitone, so that the tritone consists of B natural to F, with a low A ringing as pedal. This six-bar period, having been

Mompou, Bells and Spells

repeated, is answered with a five-bar clause with the same rune, wheedling at the same pitch like an 'antique' shepherd's pipe, over the same ostinato chord differently disposed on the keyboard. At the cadence phrase, however, the tritone doesn't subside, but is replaced by another ostinato – a low rocking between B flat and F. Throughout the coda this ostinato remains constant, withstanding softly penetrative passing dissonances. The piece doesn't end but evaporates in a silvery tinkling of bells on F, over the ostinato bass and a dominant seventh of B flat. The ultimate high B flat triad with added sixth sweetly puts 'la souffrance' to sleep, even if it isn't cured.

The second charm, *pour pénétrer les âmes*, is the most primitive of all, and perhaps needs to be, having so profoundly irrational an aim. Thematically, it consists of only five notes: E, F sharp, G, the B a third higher, returning to the G. This motif or charm is sounded, or rung bell-like, first beginning on the E in the top stave, then repeated an octave lower. It is then transposed up a fifth, sounded in octaves; and is repeated in middle register. Then it's again repeated in octaves, first at the original pitch, then an octave lower. This rune, notated in dotted minims, is accompanied by falling arpeggios in crotchets. The upper notes of each arpeggio rise up the scale in parallel sixths with the tune for its first three tones, but clash with it on a major seventh when the rune reaches its major third; the inner part ceases indeterminately on a tritone when the tune returns to G. Repeated in middle register, the theme is garlanded with chromatic bells, an open fifth ringing in the bass. The same formula is repeated for the transposed version, less thinly scored, louder. The return to the original pitch adds a quiver of broken fourths to the tollings, while the repeat at the lower octave changes the bell-chord to dominant sevenths with tritones. The last of these chords – C, A, E flat – echoes over the unchanging E minor triad. The means could hardly be more minimal; the potent effect is inverse to the minimality.

The third charm aims to inspire love, first by invoking the god, then in a love-dance of total innocence. The invocation is a

Le Jardin Retrouvé

slow chant in dotted rhythm, stepwise moving in the mixolydian mode on B flat. The 'magic chord' which, in rapid figuration, introduces and interpenetrates the chant telescopes in its arpeggios the tonic, subdominant and dominant triads of E flat minor, thereby immobilizing in a timeless moment the basic norms of progression in European music. The chant, spread over five bars, is notated in 3/4, the accompanying figuration in 3/8:

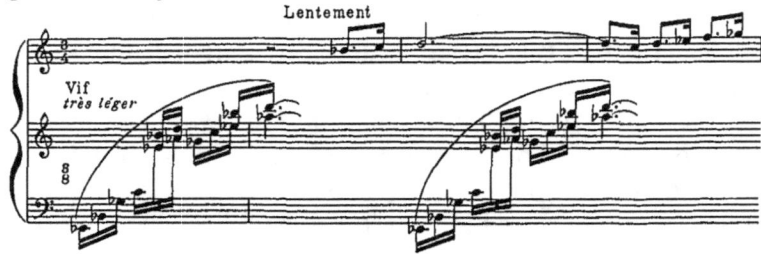

In what looks as though it will be a repeat of the tune its top note is elevated from A flat to B flat: on which crest the arpeggio shifts from E flat minor to a dominant eleventh of D flat. In this key a tiny coda-figure sinks *très calme* to rest. But the D flat changes gear abruptly, moving sharpwards to its dominant A flat major: in which occurs a rapid love-dance in 4 pulse. The accompanying figure is a shimmering of tiny bells, quivering in fourths between tonic and dominant chords; the tune, also on scintillating bells, is childishly pentatonic and symmetrical. If ever there was a music evoking a 'green paradise of childish loves', this is it; one might almost call it pre-melodic. A da capo of the invocation is unchanged except for the addition of gong-like lower octaves. The coda is very slow, making no retrospective reference to the love-dance, unless the radiant A flat major triad glowing amid the tritonal dissonances may count as such. Finally, the original E flat minorish chord is attenuated, fading into silence. Love annihilates Time.

Which is, however, the subject of the next charm, *pour évoquer l'image du passé*. Here time trudges, rather than marches, on, in an inexorable funeral march, the left hand repeating ten times an oscillation between two chords – a fragmented dominant seventh of A flat and the bare fifth A to E. The right hand's tune, in lydian B flat, recalls battles long ago through a motif of repeated notes and dotted rhythm, like a distant trumpet. The left hand ostinato is minutely changed in that the B flat at bottom of the first chord becomes B natural. This effects the tune since, although it stays at the same pitch, the Fs in the trumpet motif are sharpened. The nagging rhythm and numbing sonority don't encourage us to hear this slight shift as humanly imposed or com-posed; it sounds as though it's inflicted by the rub of Time itself – an effect reinforced by the *très rhythmé et sourd* interlude that follows: a single chord (B, G, C sharp, F sharp) throbbing like distant drums rather than bells, measuring off minutes, hours, days, years. For the da capo of the far-off military tune this same ostinato chord is substituted for the original oscillation, with a *'profond'* low E beneath, resounding like an immense gong:

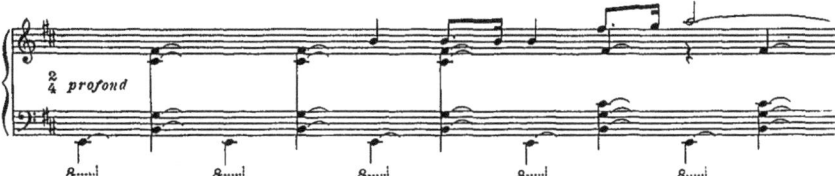

The coda carries us from history into pre-history, extending the primeval drumming. Here extreme simplicity contributes to mystery. Real savages may repeat their functional patterns ad infinitum as an accompaniment to action. When such material is presented as 'art', to be listened to privately or in a concert hall, it must be economically potent if it is to effect acts of personal therapy in our minds and senses. Mompou achieves this remarkably often, justifying his account of himself as an agent of *renouvellement*.

This certainly occurs in *pour les guérisons*, a pentatonic incantation played twice, first *clair*, then *en écho*, as though on some Panic flute. The accompaniment is a *léger* whirligig of unchanging fourths and fifths. The middle section shifts to a

Le Jardin Retrouvé

drumming ostinato between tonic and dominant of F sharp, harshly rhythmic, with a motif in parallel triads stretched to ninths. The sharpened sixths of dorian F sharp resonate mysteriously, and are not forgotten when the invocation returns da capo, for the accompaniment doesn't return to the whirligig but continues the rhythmic pattern of the middle section, telescoping triads over the dominant-tonic drums. The pentatonic tune is bell-like; the ultimate added fourths and sharp sixths *must* be campanological.

The final charm, intending to *appeler la joie*, succeeds. It opens with monody, glinting high in a dancing 6 8, in pentatonic B or A – the centre is ambiguous. The exiguous texture, notated on one stave, sounds like a child's cascading laughter: another instance of maximum effect from minimal means:

This cry covers six *gai* bars: after which the music doesn't modulate but simply shifts gear to C sharp major, in which key we hear a *ludus puerorum* in a rapidly flickering 3 8. All those seven sharps shine – as they did in *Secreto* from *Impresiones Intimas* – like Henry Vaughan's 'white Celestiall Thought' in the Garden of Eden, the rune noodling around the fifth, with a sparkling accompaniment of broken sevenths and ninths in middle register. We hear Vaughan's 'Bright Shootes of everlastingness' tingling through 'all this fleshly dresse'; the music may even approximate to Traherne's famous vision of the Golden City of Childhood in his *Centuries of Meditation:*

> Boyes and Girles Tumbling in the Street, and Playing, were moving Jewels. I knew not that they were Born or should Die . . . Eternity was manifest in the Light of Day . . . The Citty seemed to stand in Eden, or to be built in Heaven. The Streets were mine, the Temple was mine, the People were mine, their Clothes and Gold and Silver were mine, and I the only Spectator and Enjoyer of it. I knew no Churlish

Mompou, Bells and Spells

Proprieties, nor Bounds, nor Divisions . . . so that with much Adoe I was corrupted, and made to learn the Dirty Devices of this World. Which now I unlearn, and become as it were a little Child again, that I may enter into the Kingdom of God.

This is the closest Mompou comes to the Edenic vision of our 17th century Nature mystic; and his consciousness of the Fall is discreetly manifest even in the second half of this dance, for the modally flattened sixth and seventh of the scale prepare the ground for the darker middle section in 2 4, with whole-tone oscillations over a B-F sharp ostinato. The relatively harsh sonority dissolves in chromatics as the ostinato drums peter out; the paradisal *ludus puerorum* doesn't recur. And although the babbling child's laughter comes back as coda, its effect is changed, since it's supported by an ostinato of fourths over a pedal F sharp. The final echoing chord rings these fourths over a fifth, F sharp to C sharp; the lack of resolution, combined with the teetering in the drumming section, makes us aware that the joy so delightfully summoned is precarious. Each *renouvellement* occurs in St. Paul's twinkling of an eye; as Blake put it, 'He who catches a joy *as it flies* Lives in eternity's sunrise'. There may be a parallel with Satie's melancholy-merry clowns, acrobats and jugglers, poised over a small abyss.

Along with these piano pieces we may group, as charms and incantations, a set of four songs to Mompou's own Catalan texts, published a decade later in 1931, though they were composed between 1925 and 1928. The words of the first song, *Rosa del Camí,* are as magical as they are minimal: 'sweetly fading in the night   beneath a tree   fell a star   in the morning I found a rose in my path'. *Très calme,* the song unfolds, flower-like, over a pedal E and an ostinato pentatonic chord of E, F sharp, A and B. The piano part is tranquil bells; the vocal part is chant rather than song, always in middle register, undulating around a nodal point, B or A. Movement is mainly by step; the only intervals traversed are pentatonic minor thirds and fourths. Often the piano silvers the vocal line at the unison

Le Jardin Retrouvé

or octave; caressing chromatic passing notes creep into the cadential phrases. As in *Cants magics* and *Charmes,* there is no harmonic and little melodic and rhythmic movement as the music tries to recapture that 'everlasting feeling' which, according to Gertrude Stein, 'broken man yearns for'.

Cortina de fullatge is less incantatory than the slow-swinging censer of *Rosa del camí,* but opens in faintly liturgical canon in aeolian A flat, shifting up a semitone to glimpse the magic moon through an Edenic 'curtain of leaves'. The melody consists of chanted repeated notes alternating with stepwise movement, hypnotically accompanied by homophonically chromatized chords over a dotted rhythm. From its initial flat regions the song sidles back to the incantation, now in dorian B minor, ending with a piano postlude that unfolds the curtain of leaves in overlapping arpeggios – fifths and fourths in the right hand, a B minor triad with added sharp sixth in the left:

Incertitud is really about incertitude's opposite, since it concerns the truth of love within the heart, overriding uncertain external perils. Like the first song, it opens with an ostinato bell-chord, though instead of rudimentary pentatonics we have a linking of two neutral, and to that degree unstable, tritones. The vocal line is pitched higher than usual with Mompou, elevating chant to song of primal simplicity. The first four-bar phrase is pentatonic on E, but the answering three bars entwine chromatics into a descent from B to G. The piano's bells also garner chromatics through sharply penetrative, rather than luscious, seventh chords; a piano postlude again enfolds the vocal chant in a haze of broken arpeggios, the voice's original pentatonic line ringing through whole-tone insubstantiality.

Mompou, Bells and Spells

The low B at the bottom of the arpeggios is a reverberating gong.

The last song, *Neu,* enters another dimension: spiritually, because the poem, far from being a dream, evokes snow as the traditional image of death, while presenting snow-flakes as flowers, a crown to life; and technically, because it graduates from incantation or rune to *song,* and exists in temporality – between life and death. Though it begins in 'instinctive' pentatonicism, darkly accompanied by minor triads over an E flat pedal, it does have beginning, middle and end, and effects an equilibrium between the communal (the melody, lifting through a minor third, then arching stepwise, is as apparently spontaneous as a folk song) and the personal (the inner parts within the piano's chords point the melody with expressive chromatics):

So although the song, snow-drugged, resembles the other songs in inducing trance through its 'inevitable' melody and numbing rhythm, it also embraces personal awareness of life and death. Its delicately penetrative dissonances, like snow and ice, burn as they freeze; the music has no need of the 'added notes' that in Mompou's music, as in Debussy's and Ravel's, often betoken nostalgia. On the phrase *Ai, quina tristesa* the vocal line

Le Jardin Retrouvé

peters out, wavering between the 'instinctive' fourth and fifth, while the piano is left with bare octave E flats, dropping with snow's gentle remorselessness. This haunting little song is the first example we have lighted on of the essential Mompou *melody*, as distinct from rune or incantation. The nature of these melodies, and of Mompou's response to the human voice, will be considered in a later chapter. *Neu* carries us beyond our immediate concern, which is Mompou's *pre*-melodic, even pre-conscious magic. We will round the chapter off by looking at a piano work, dating from 1920, wherein Mompou makes a transition from magic into *festivity*, which is not a spell or a charm, but generates an aura in which magic may flourish. Mompou called this set of six small pieces *Fêtes lointaines*.

In religious ceremonial and secular festivity at any time and place, even in our post-industrial world, we may be released from linear, chronometric time and re-enter circular or mythological time wherein, as Octavio Paz has put it, 'time is not succession and transition but rather the perpetual sound of a fixed present in which all times, past, present and future, are contained . . . Man, the prisoner of succession, breaks out of his invisible jail and enters living time; his subjective life becomes identical with exterior time, because this has ceased to be a spatial measurement and has changed into a source, a spring, in the absolute present, endlessly repeating itself. Myths and fiestas, whether secular or religious, permit man to emerge from his solitude and become one with creation . . . Myth opens the doors of communion'.

Mompou's festivals, like those of Debussy in his orchestral *Fêtes*, are significantly *lointain* – distant in time and perhaps in space. At the age of twenty-seven, he seems to be remembering them from childhood as much as from a village community: there is no clear distinction between these *Fêtes lointaines* and the childhood pieces to be considered in the next chapter. No. 1 begins with bells similar to those in the magic pieces, the first ten-bar period consisting of repetitions of a B flat pedal with piled-up fourths and fifths above it, swaying pendulum-like

Mompou, Bells and Spells

between octaves; if a grammatical explanation is needed, this might be construed as an aeolian B flat chord with minor ninth as unresolved appoggiatura. Through these tolling bells rings a pentatonic incantation, floating directionless on their reverberations. Tempo suddenly changes to 6 8, *gai,* for a frolicking kiddies' game with an arpeggiated tune in lydian E flat, accompanied by an E flat triad in first inversion, the key note of which occasionally flickers to E natural (which equals F flat):

The effect is pert, saucy in more than one sense; but after another ten bars the game dissipates over a tonic-dominant pedal, with expressive dissonances. There's a characteristic equilibrium between the cocky impudence of the playing children and the grown young man's watching eye and listening ear: which may be why the da capo of the game-dance, with perkier figuration and a slightly less static accompaniment, sounds wistful, the sighing dissonances are more protracted, and in a coda the fourth-pervaded aeolian B flat sinks to a pentatonic D flat, *plus clair.* The festivities expire in pentatonic bells.

The second *fête* also glitters with bells, this time silverily tinkling. Semiquavers oscillate between fourth and seventh over a pedal A, with a symmetrical children's game motif in the alto. Fourths are again omnipresent. In the ninth bar the bells cease and the mode shifts from aeolian A with flat fifth to dorian D. After a repeat an octave higher, there's a 'middle' with an incantatory rune again like a kids' game, over a pedal, now syncopated, on D and A. There is only one minor third in the first four bars but when, in bar 5, major thirds make the mode mixolydian, the rudimentary tune is irradiated. In a repeat D sharp is substituted for the F sharp of the fifth bar; changes

Le Jardin Retrouvé

enharmonically to E flat; and so leads to a da capo of the first section.

In the third *fête* contrast is overt between the vivacity of the duple-rhythmed dance, which is pentatonic on A and sounds folk-like as well as childish, and the expressivity of the cadences' appoggiaturas. There are four bars of dance, two of cadence; both are repeated over a pedal A, with percussively unresolved double appoggiaturas. The 'crying' cadence is also modified, becoming a German sixth. The middle is more songful, in dotted rhythm, though the fourth and fifth pervaded harmony remains gong-like. As in the previous piece, and recurrently in Mompou's music, there's a contrast between the hedonistic 'present moment' of fiesta and the age-old, yet also personal and private, lament of the cadences. We and Mompou at once belong to, and are separated from, these communal satisfactions: little boys with noses pressed against the sweetshop window. This dichotomy becomes more potent, even disturbing, in the fourth *fête*, which juxtaposes an innocently white-note dance-game over an A pedal with a triple-rhythmed answering clause in dotted metre, over gently percussive bells in a reiterated chord of E, F and A. When the dance-game is repeated, its 12 8 pedal note changes from A to G, though the white-note figuration remains the same. This possibly shifts the modality to mixolydian, and certainly affects the coda-restatement of the second clause, now poised over a deep pedal E, and more melodically folk-like, with quintuplet arabesques, leading into dissonant unresolved appoggiaturas. The 'outsider' is not just a little boy, for Mompou's darker gypsy, with a whiff of Moorish flamenco, has reared his haunting head:

At the end the bells and gongs also suggest the twang of gypsy guitar.

Mompou, Bells and Spells

The folk flavour of this piece may have prompted Mompou to conceive the next *fête* as a *Cançó i dansa* comparable with his main series of folk-derived works, to be discussed in a later chapter. The song, in dorian G, has parallel 6 3 chords swaying in dotted rhythm over bell-like tonics and dominants; the dance is in diatonic G major, *très gai,* with a bass alternating between dominant and subdominant. The upper parts, though still in parallel 6 3 chords, are merry rather than mournful; there is again hardly a tune, only rhythm and texture. The 'middle', *un peu plus doux,* insinuates discreet chromatic passing notes, which in the restatement of the first clause become bouncily percussive. The Song is heard da capo, unchanged except that the tune is now in the alto, haloed by seventh chords; and although in a brief coda the dance resounds at its original rapid tempo, it does so in echo, its jollity now dream-like, if not illusory. Something similar happens in the final *fête,* with a tune of rocking fourths and fifths in C major, with white note 6 3 chords supporting it in a very fast 3 8 — a time signature Mompou seems to associate with Edenic junketing, as in the C sharp major section of the charme *pour appeler la joie.* The middle section, mostly in parallel fourths over a C-G drone, allows no quiver of personal expressivity to sully this Edenic mindlessness, though again the coda prevents our taking this at its face value, for the repeat — *très loin, comme un écho* — comes from another world or a distant past.

That past is, of course, childhood, from which Mompou, at twenty-seven, was still not all that far removed. We've noted how in the game-like pieces in *Fêtes lointaines* he demonstrates how magic flourishes in the secret garden of childhood and is threatened as we timidly step into the wide world. But his music also tells us how magic may become a means whereby we attempt to grow up. As we pass, in Geza Roheim's words, 'through the pregenital to the genital phase of organization and as, concurrently, our mastery of our own body and of the environment increases', magic, with its source in the hallucinatory wish-fulfilments of the infant, becomes 'an invocation of

Le Jardin Retrouvé

our own natures'. Without it, we cannot believe in our identities; and without such trust, we cannot 'hold our own against the environment'. Rites of passage are our magical attempts to resist, and at the same time to cope with, change, celebrating the transitions from birth to infancy, from childhood to puberty, from manhood to marriage, from age to death. These rites children act out in their singing and dancing games: on which some of Mompou's most centrally representative pieces are based.

IV

Mompou's 'Ludi Puerorum'

The child is all that is abandoned and exposed and at the same time divinely powerful: the insignificant, dubious beginning, and the triumphant end. The 'eternal child' in man is an indescribable experience, an incongruity, a disadvantage, and a divine prerogative; an imponderable that determines the ultimate worth or worthlessness of a personality.

JUNG: *Essays on a Science of Mythology*

Babies love only themselves
and think the world is there for them.
Children are selfish
and learn only slowly not to grasp and grab.
Even the cutest kid
is far less Ego than Id . . .

Yet they *have*
an innocence, they're honest,
the one thing they can't do is pretend,
infants speak true,
what they feel they certainly show.
They're not divine –
but they're not hypocritical swine.

GAVIN EWART

Fun and gravity are sisters.

PLATO: *Epistulae 6*

MAGIC is endemic in the experience of the child who, a small savage, resembles his primitive forebears in making song and dance to bolster the security surrendered when he left the mother's womb. Once he's out in the world, sprouting through infancy to childhood, he sings and dances with his peers, both as an attempt to mythologize his lost womb-like state, and as a means of making the unknown amenable, or at least less inimical. Music and dance, usually associated with incantatory verse, provide for children an activity outside life, in a sense not 'serious', yet intensely and utterly absorbing. Temporarily – as Erik Erikson has demonstrated – normal life is suspended as we enter the Sacred Place within which we play under fixed unalterable rules, often with disguise to separate the in-group from the world outside. We speak of 'playing' music, and the word 'illusion' derives from the Latin *in lusione,* in play: in which sense children indulge in fiesta and ceremonial, creating art, but not 'works of' art, which can occur only when we accept the burden of consciousness unequivocally. The work metaphor makes a point, in contrast to the ever present activity of *homo ludens.*

In Britain the rediscovery and collation of children's singing games was initiated in the late nineteenth century by Lady Alice Gomme, wife of an anthropologist, and therefore eager to rescue the games from the veneer of Victorian sanctimoniousness. Since then, we have learned much more about them, largely through the work of the redoubtable Peter and Iona Opie;* and have come to realize that what makes the games so fascinating is that they function on at least four levels. From the dark backward and abysm of time springs the Jungian archetypal dimension which children, creatures of instinct, admit without the prevarications of guilt or remorse. Nearer the surface are survivals of the archetypes transmitted in folk plays, festivities, and ballads, the stylized language of which – lilywhite hands, silver cups, long golden hair – crop up, often in reference to movie stars and pop stars, in the dreariest industrial suburb. With these legendary elements meld specific historical events which seemed significant when contemporary, but which

* This section on children's games incorporates material from my Times Literary Supplement review of the Opie's *The Singing Game,* and is vicariously indebted to that wonderful book.

Mompou's 'Ludi Puerorum'

with the passage of time have become intertangled, wildly regardless of chronological sequence, and in effect often legendary themselves. Finally there's the level of here and now, in our street or village; immediately contemporary experience given enhanced import through being seen in relation to mythology and history – which it at the same time cuts down to size.

For evidence one need look no further than some of the most famous, still current, singing games. Consider how children luminously confront, even when they're very young, the facts of love and death, as they act out 'Poor Jenny (or Mary or Sally or Sarah) lies a-weeping'. When they're only a little older they're intuitively more aware – as in the mysteriously titled 'Green Gravel' which so mesmerized Thomas Hardy – how precarious the balance between creation and destruction must be. Yet more subtly equivocal is 'Wallflowers, wallflowers', which seems to be a funerary rite for maidens who are 'sure to die', yet is also, having assimilated a game with the doubly acqueous title of 'Sally Waters', a well-building as well as wall-falling ceremony, evoking the watery wellsprings of life. Death is symbolized by the magic circle dancing, rather sedately, with backs to the dying maiden; but the resurrection at the end, facing forwards, is spiritual renewal rather than wish-fulfilment. That the death-dance and well-blessing had separate origins only makes their marriage in the children's game the more mysterious.

These games are now played almost exclusively by girls; boys are even reluctant to participate in the innumerable courtship and wedding games, of which the most widespread is 'Nuts in May', and the many rites involving (often ribaldly) cushions. Anthropologists and folklorists sound pretentious when pointing out, however justly, the relations of these games to communally sanctioned match-making and to primitive fertility rites; yet although the children don't know with their conscious minds what they're doing, they certainly know in their nerves and senses, or they would hardly have found the games worth preserving. For 'unconscious' children those four levels of

Le Jardin Retrouvé

experience coexist. In 'Oats and beans' they don't recognize that they're prancing around in a spring festival, but they do sense that they're involved in something strangely life-enhancing. In the related game 'The farmer's in his den' thoughtful youngsters may be puzzled by that den which, oblivious of the medieval meaning, they tend to relate to Daniel and his lions, thereby adding to the story a layer which, if irrational, is not non-sensical. Similarly, in playing the contest game 'Romans and English', kids would guffaw at the historian's gloss that the contest is that of the Roman and Anglican Church, which is supposed to explain the reference to bread and wine. They'd be on the mark, however, in recognizing that contest between goodies and baddies is an ineradicable human instinct which may be momently absolved in mirth and buffoonery, as well as acted out in acrimony and violence. Crazy comedy is often a child's way of dealing with things he's conscious enough to know he can't consciously assimilate: for instance the farcical doctors promoting resurrections, whom he shares with medieval folk drama, or the rude sexual jokes about puddings which he shares with the black blues: not to mention those 'four Jews from Spain' who corruptly and perhaps corruptingly insinuate themselves into a 'simple' game of courtship. They may be more fearful than funny, yet are also good for a slightly nervous giggle. On the whole, the child has a healthy suspicion of transcendentalism, without denying its potentiality. The Opies report that a little girl playing 'Fair Rosie' – a quite modern permutation of the Sleeping Beauty story – chanted the title with poetic relish, yet didn't hold with the suggestion that the Prince ought to kiss the Princess awake: 'Nope; we just gives 'er a shove'.

There's a similar deflatory element in many of the mating games; 'you shall get a duke, my dear, and *you* shall get a drake' is a joke genuinely witty because unexpected. A child could invent it any day, and it would be 'modern' yet also relevant to days when dukes were Dukes, and perhaps related to many nun- and monk-mocking games which may – since kids nowadays don't bother overmuch about ecclesiastical hierarchies — hark back to the medieval Feast of Fools. Many perplexing nonsense refrains manage simultaneously to debunk and to open vistas. Mostly they're gibberish because they belong to an oral tradition which, in the nature of things, is subject to corruption. A wedding game, 'Merry-ma-tansie', sung to the tune of 'Nuts in May', offers a literally enthralling instance. According to the etymologists, 'merry ma tansie' may be a corruption of 'merry maids dancing', or of the German 'Mit mir tanzen', or even of 'matanza', a ceremonial pig-sticking in Spain. More cosily, it may derive from the Glasgow version 'And round about Mary Matansy' (equals 'matins say'!): which might explain why the girls sometimes curtsey (in homage to God's mother) instead of clumping to the ground. The mystery and poetry lie in the fact that children know, even if etymologists don't, that these and many other meanings aren't mutually exclusive.

Of course, not all children's games have mythic dimensions. Many are simple action games, serving to release adrenalin; many deal with the everyday realities of a humdrum life, destructively yet comically enlivened by drunken dads and cantankerous mums. Some pantomine songs, such as 'Mary is a bad girl', accept the grim facts of life and death with brusque insouciance; others dramatize, and perhaps anneal, petty squabbles and dissensions. A few are glumly educational, as the ubiquitous 'Here we go round the mulberry bush' became in Victorian times, whatever it may once have been as a tree-circling ceremony. At any level, however, children's games are sanity incarnate, compared with the criminal imbecilities of the adult world. Seventeenth century grown-ups, serving their monstrous God, forbade children to play games like the wondrous 'Green gravel' and 'Wallflowers' on the grounds that the backward-facing circle must be a witches sabbath, conducive to licentiousness. The only barbarity was in their denunciation; and before we congratulate ourselves on the fact that this was in the bad old days, we should recall that a fairly recent 'interpretation' of the best loved of all round games, 'Ring a ring

Le Jardin Retrouvé

o' roses', is that it's about the plague of 1685, the roses being plague sores, the tishoos the sneezes alleged to accompany the disease, the falling down the ultimate declension of death! Mercifully children – even the toughest urban types – still know that roses are flowers of love, the circle holistic magic.

Fortunately there is nothing that adult commentators, however learned, can do about the music to the games, for the tunes are of a pristine simplicity that has never had need of notation. True, a few derive from written music-hall and pop tunes which, if strong enough, may hang on long after the topical ingredients, and even the names of the pop stars associated with them, have gone the way of all flesh. It's interesting that the majority of 'traditional' tunes, of uncertain antiquity and usually transmitted orally, are plain diatonic major. This doesn't indicate that they are corruptions of modal originals but rather that the ionian mode (equivalent to our modern major scale) is most apposite to childhood's childishness. This seems to apply regardless of geographical location, though the most 'primitive' runes tend to reduce diatonic major to a basic pentatonicism. Even the briefest rune has survived because it's memorable; the songs with the profoundest overtones and undertones, like 'Green gravel' and 'Wallflowers', tend to have the most haunting melodies. The magical effect of the bride song 'Rosie apple', for instance, seems to be due to the way in which the tune, at first confined within the tones of a major triad, opens out to waft skywards in a triad on the subdominant. The skipping girls may blow kisses, on this lilting subdominant, to the 'lilywhite' maid, leading her 'across the water'. The Opies have produced iconographical evidence that this has been, and is still being, enacted, with astonishing equivalence, by children and young people at various times from the Middle Ages onwards, in various places throughout Europe and America: almost certainly in Catalonia – a fact which links our experience of our own childhoods with the magical encapsulation of childhood games in Mompou's music.

This may partially explain why Mompou's first 'childhood'

Mompou's 'Ludi Puerorum'

piece, *Scènes d'enfants,* composed between 1915 and 1918, has become his most performed and probably best loved work. It touches us on the raw, belonging to *us* more directly than do the magic pieces, which uncover primeval impulses we've come near to forgetting. *Scènes d'enfants* offers a vision of Eden the more poignant because it is – unlike the dancing *charme* wherein Mompou summons joy – tinged with regret.

The pieces in *Scènes d'enfants* are all *ludi,* and it's significant that the first is called *Cris dans la rue*: this game is urban, in the streets of what was then, in 1915, modern Barcelona. The first section, marked '*gai*', is adrenalin-releasing action music, without 'personal' expressivity, as blissfully Edenic as the dance in the '*Joie*' *charme.* In a fast, swinging triple pulse, it consists of chords made of piled-up, 'primitive' because non-triadic, fourths:

In their undeviating 'whiteness' these fourths are both perfect and imperfect (tritonal): so that in medieval terminology both God (whose interval was the absolute consonance of the perfect fourth and its inversion the fifth) and the Devil (whose interval was the tritone) are simultaneously present. *Si contra fa diabolus est,* said the ancient rubric; and one can hardly expect 'pre-conscious' children to be very clear about distinctions between right and wrong. Nor should we be surprised that the noise sounds like merrily chiming bells which clatter on regardless of human principles and priorities, and also like the inarticulate yells of birds, beasts, and small human creatures not far from an animal state. At first the symmetrical clause is all fourths in both hands, but it's repeated with the fourths in the right hand, accompanied by a syncopated drone on the open fifth of C. Possibly the syncopation imparts a hint of unease to the bird-like blitheness; certainly the dance-game fades and diminishes.

It's followed by another dance, marked *très vif*, which may be faster than *gai*, and is certainly perkier. The *gai* prelude is relatively inchoate childish hubbub; in the *très vif* the kids are organizing themselves in the simplest of round games, having modulated sharpwards to the dominant – an unambiguous diatonic G major (or the ionian mode on G) over an unchanging tonic-dominant ostinato in the left hand. Whereas the first section consists only of *cris* and tintinnabulations, this section has a defined tune which children might whistle in the street; although the tune itself – as distinct from its tonic-dominant harmonization – is innocently pentatonic, it is, in its metrical regularity, urban street-song rather than rural folk-song. The first section is merriment *in essentia*, happy yet also sad against the backcloth of the city and of time and eternity; whereas the G major round-dance, diatonically down to earth, animates specific children in a brief here-and-now. From this 'moment' emerges a little love song, *calme*, growing from the undulations of the G major dance but harmonizing its lyricism with the parallel fourths and tonic-dominant drone of the first section. Though we don't know this when we first hear the melody, it is to be the song of the *jeunes filles au jardin* of the last movement. The *jardin* is of course Eden; but *jeunes filles* suggests adolescence and the Fall: which must be why Mompou advises the performer to 'chanter un peu grossièrement'. Although the tune is full of promise and bloom, a *contrepartie* notated on a separate stave points it with an occasional tingling dissonance.

And the song doesn't last long, dissolving mistily into a da capo of the original dance, now marked *gai*, but also *lointain*. The far-off-ness implies that the child's experience is viewed, even by young Mompou, with a measure of retrospection; growing up, like those *jeunes filles*, he may nostalgically relish the golden days of childhood which – as the episodic structure of the piece indicates – were one blessed, rather than damned,

Mompou's 'Ludi Puerorum'

thing after another. At the end gentle appoggiaturas turn into distant bells in the still air – twilight, one hazards, as compared with the shining morn of the first section.

The next three pieces are all called *Jeu*, and happen *sur la plage*, where children are frolicking with the eternal sea as backcloth. The pathos of the music – one may get a similar frisson from the beach scenes of the painter Boudin – springs from the contrast between the bustle of the present moment and the eternal unconsciousness of the sea as the womb from which we come, the tomb into which we dissipate. The first sounds we hear are labelled *cri*: and might be the labour-cry of birth itself, as well as the spontaneous yells of children on the sands. In either guise these *cris*, here and throughout the piece, have startling verisimilitude, though a percussive and equal tempered piano is far from the acoustic properties of a crying Spanish juvenile. The reason must be that Mompou evokes the scene so vividly that our aural imagination supplies the timbres the piano lacks. This initial *cri* is a brief yell of a dominant seventh of C major with an added A flat, the latter functioning as though it were G sharp in false relation with the G natural of an E minor triad. The *cri* sounds wild, animal-like or at least not quite human; but when the game proper starts it is rhythmic and metrically regular, unexpectedly marked *tranquillement*. The tune, in four-bar periods, undulates between B, A and C; is answered by a pentatonic phrase starting on the D a third higher; and is rounded off by a repeat of the original clause. The tonic to this rune is ambivalent. The right hand harmonizes the melodic undulations with a fourth and then fifth, D to G, C to G, the second chord containing a dissonant seventh. The droning pedal notes and the tonal ambiguity give the music a tranced dreaminess – as though it's aware of a gulf between the young, near-animal desperation of those ephemeral *cris* and the eternal immensity of the ocean, whose subacqueous murmur the piano emulates. Though the second clause on D, harmonized in parallel fourths and fifths, is a shade jauntier, this only makes the da capo of the first clause the more wistful: as is

Le Jardin Retrouvé

spelled out in the coda, marked *douloureux*, when the false relation latent in the original *cris* becomes patent in the harmonic cadence. The piece ends, or stops, where it started, with the abruptly vulnerable *cris*, which never have a dynamic marking. The last sound is a 'white' ninth chord on A, echoing into silence; we understand now why the piece's 'tranquillity' is oddly disturbing:

Mompou's *cris*, being almost pre-articulate, are not straight diatonic major like the game-tunes, but are in variously altered modality. The *cri* that opens the second *jeu*, for instance, consists of a descending tritone, G sharp to D natural, at first solo, then with an underpinning of G sharp, E and A sharp. The rune-tune is a 'cell' of these four notes: a mode which sounds slightly distraught over the bass's beating ostinato. The clause, lasting six bars, is answered by a five-bar phrase a fifth higher, beneath which the sixths of the accompanying quavers move chromatically. The tritonal *cri* is itself harsh, gamin-like and, in its 'altered' modality, gypsyish: which may prompt the relative agitation of the harmony, as compared with the sea-murmuring background to the first piece. But after a chromatic cadence-phrase the sea comes into its own, in a passage marked *très vif*, but also *sourd*. Tune, or even cry, disappears, and an ostinato of fifths on G sharp and E, shifted in the third bar to a tritone, pounds in incipient violence. The sea subsides and the human *cri* comes back, marked *triste*, and sounding irremediably forlorn. Yet the piece ends not in fade-out, but with a full G sharp minor triad: a bit stark, as though these gamins have their resilience:

Mompou's 'Ludi Puerorum'

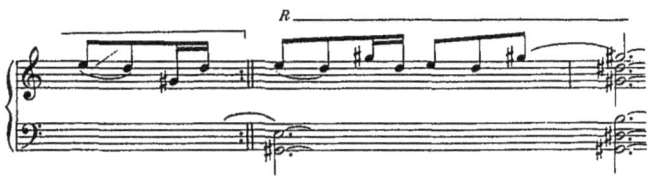

The third *jeu* opens with a sharp juxtaposition of boy and sea. The *cri* is a wriggle between E and D, over an open fifth E to B; it's followed in bass register by a reverberating tritone, B *flat* to E natural, marked *'profond'*. The game, in a *vif* 3/8, fuses both elements, for the tune is another stepwise noodling around the tonic E but then pushing impudently up the scale, accompanied by an ostinato B flat with rather fierce appoggiaturas. In the eighth bar it disperses in three repetitions of an appoggiatura F sharp to E above a G minor triad: which floats into distant recollections of the original *cri,* now called *interrogation,* as though the boy – wondering what's the point of our human games, and who has won, anyway – were listening for the unknowable sea's unheard answer:

When the game-tune resumes an octave lower the left hand figuration embroiders the tritones the piece had started from. Although they have a slightly serpentine energy and may hint at gypsyish devilment, they rotate on themselves rather than 'going' anywhere. This must be why, when the game-tune stops, the tritonal bass becomes an ostinato on C instead of E, with a gently falling 'tumbling strain' on top. This tune is marked *très triste*; all that juvenile bounciness doesn't, it seems, count for much in sight or hearing of the eternal sea. The *jeu* disperses in a distant wriggling of the original *cri* a tone higher. Mompou says *Questionnez au loin*; but after only a brief silence the kids on the

Le Jardin Retrouvé

beach give themselves a shake, like puppies, and return to their tritone-infested game in its low, bassoon-like register, somewhat louder and perhaps a shade aggressive. The appoggiatura fade-out is succeeded by a questioning repetition of the preludial *cri* and the sepulchral tritone. The final sound is a plain E minor triad, with a cavernous low E.

Miraculously, Mompou manages to suggest that this is an epitome of the human lot – as Schubert often does in the irremediably final minor triad to a song.

The final piece, *Jeunes filles au jardin,* is placed last because, after the pieces about childhood's eternal present, it hints at growing up and at the sexuality inherent in the process. The garden, although Edenic, is a real one, perhaps to a town house in sight and sound of the sea: which is initially evoked in a *calme,* tenderly floating dominant seventh of E flat with an unresolved double appoggiatura on E flat and C flat, suspended in the still air. The young girls break the spell by skipping in leaping octaves, with clinking acciacaturaed tritones; though after a bar and a half they change from hoydens to young ladies, dancing in ceremonial graciousness, still in 6 8, but *calme* and *très doux*. The calm is deceptive, for although the tune undulates up and down the scale of E flat over a sweetly swaying pedal B flat, it soon loses its moorings as the harmony floats through G flat major, C minor, B flat major, G minor, and so back to E flat. Though the effect is dreamy, such volatile tonality is atypical of Mompou's magic and childhood pieces, and must surely be related to the young things' burgeoning sexuality. A trifle fearful, they break off their moony meanderings to return to their childish (but tritonal!) antics with the skipping rope, the preludial leaping octaves being now *gai* as well as *vif*. But this scamper is over almost as soon as it's started; the girls return to their dreaming, now in the form of a hopefully fulfilled love song, of which we'd been given intimation in the first piece of the cycle. Then it had been simply harmonized, mostly in fourths, even though Mompou had asked us to sing it *un peu grossièrement*; now it carols *avec la fraîcheur de l'herbe humide*, and its harmony is chromatically rich, if diaphanously spaced:

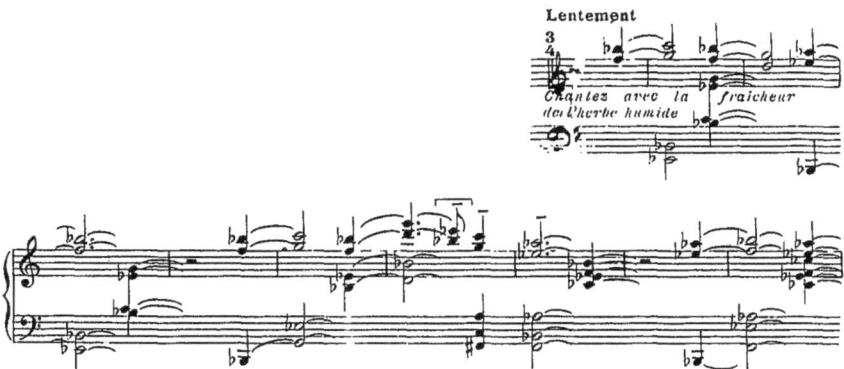

This is not a chant but a real melody, on the way to an adult song, with the stepwise movement of the earlier 'gracious' tune expanding invitingly into a rising sixth. Wide-spaced chromatic harmonies point the crests of the phrases in ways that suggest the jazz pianism of Bill Evans or Chick Correa, neither of whom was born at the time the piece was written. This makes sense, for in both Mompou and the jazzmen seductively Latin American rhythms and delicately luscious harmonies balance between vernal promise and regret. Duke Ellington too – not to mention art composers such as Gershwin, Delius and Ravel who were concerned with similar ranges of experience – sings (in Allen Ginsberg's words) of 'nostalgias of another life, mythologies he cannot inherit'. Mompou was closer to folk sources than were the Europeans and the American in their industrial cities, but the parallel holds. This theme will be further explored in considering Mompou works specifically concerned with adolescence.

Le Jardin Retrouvé

In this *scène d'enfants* the premonition of growing up is fleeting: which is why those pianists who, loving the tune and wishing it were longer, repeat it, may be misguided. True, Mompou himself does so in his recorded performance; even so, that he doesn't *indicate* a repeat may make a point, since the love-song's vernal promise is tentative; even when it happens, if it happens, it will be lost in a transient moment. Not surprisingly, these *jeunes filles* are distinguished from the other pieces in the sequence in that they have little affinity with Satie's middle period music of childhood. True, between Satie and Mompou in his children's musics there is a general parallel: both, like real children, use short, repetitive phrases in quasi-geometric patterns, which tend to be diatonic or in white note modality. But Satie's childhood pieces are devoid of Mompou's discreet 'added' notes and overtones, let alone his jazzy chromatics: consequently, they are without nostalgia. Similarly, Ravel sings as an adult of childhood lost: whereas Satie, who said 'Je suis venu au monde très jeune dans un temps très vieux', momentarily *becomes* a child. Though Mompou's music looks more like Satie's than Ravel's it is more Ravellian in spirit. He has a simple heart and an innocent eye and ear but knows that, in growing to man's estate, he must regretfully put away childish things, while never forgetting the magic they don't 'represent' but are. This is evident in another early piano work, the *Suburbis* of 1916–17, which, while making no explicit reference to childhood, sees and hears the urban or suburban world through a child's eye and ear.

Interestingly, these pieces are dedicated *à ma mère*, as young Mompou enters, without exactly confronting, the wider world. The first piece, *La rue, le guitariste et le vieux cheval*, is by far Mompou's longest thus far, and is so *because* it's about the town 'out there'. Structurally, it's a sequence of 'scenes', unfolding yet coexistent, like life itself – in this case just one thing, neither damned nor blessed, after another. A twiddling of four semiquavers around a nodal B flat with a pentatonic (in fact only three-note) call above it, suggests bustling activity,

Mompou's 'Ludi Puerorum'

perhaps another street game. With a shift to a rapid 3 8 a gamin-like tune, *sifflant avec indifférence*, floats between tonic and fifth over vacillating chords of B flat minor and D flat dominant seventh in second inversion, with an unchanging B flat as pedal. False relations between triads of E flat and C majors slightly sting the insouciance, until there's a real modulation to G flat major by way of sensuously spaced chromatics marked *sensible*. Mompou tells us that the new tune, which is however related to the gamin-tune, is a *valse*; although a *valse*-like step – or a step and a hop, the free foot crossed over the stepping foot – is typical of much Catalan folk dance, this is clearly street café-music, intermittently interrupted by flickering cadenzas in major seconds, emulating the street guitar player. The piece unfolds in mirror form, two statements of the valse being capped by a da capo of the whistling gamin: which in turn fades, *plus lent*, into a da capo of the bustling semiquavers, now harmonized with an E flat major triad. Morning zest is compromised by the coda, which begins *très lent*, with hypnotic dominant sevenths of F flat or E (the notation is enharmonic), pierced by sharp acciacaturas, marked *péniblement*:

This must be the *vieux cheval*, suffering as, in this piece, human creatures don't. The end, if end it be, is very *lointain*. The scurrying semiquavers recur, far off, over a bell-like E flat chord with added sixth. It's as though the watching eye and listening ear are part of the suburban scene, yet detached from it. This is why the piece is so much subtler, and more moving, than the aural picture-postcard it might have been.

It is to the point that in the next two pieces Mompou evokes gypsies, perennial outsiders with a mysterious and alien ancestry who, as Peter Whigham has put it, 'live outside Church and

Le Jardin Retrouvé

village, who dance round the fire, Eat crab-apples raw . . .

> Not rich and not poor, on the crab-apple moor,
> With a wisdom all of their own,
> Their humility may
> Well have something to say
> When the rats shall their rat-race disown.

Gypsies had something of this import even in the cosier reaches of 19th century culture – in, for instance, the violin concerto and clarinet quintet of Brahms, as well as in the more extrovert play-acting of Liszt. We may recall too the gypsies who in Delius's *A Village Romeo and Juliet* lure the child lovers to those waterily unconscious Paradise Gardens which offer, even if only in death, truths other than the 'Dirty Devices' (Traherne's phrase) of a corruptly mercantile society. Mompou's gypsies aren't glamorized like those of the 19th century romantics but they too, in being outsiders, offer glimpses over the horizon of the known and knowable. Their music sounds, in Mompou's gypsy pieces, as they must look: dark, even dirty, lean, gaunt, 'other'. It is worth noting that as late as the mid nineteen thirties Violet Alford witnessed in the Vallès district, about thirty kilometres north of Barcelona, a carnival Dance of the Gypsies which symbolizes their equivocal nature, for it is at once a fertility rite celebrating the union of a gypsy bride and groom, and a dramatization of territorial squabbles, with the 'locals' defending their land against the aliens. The intruders are glamorously flower-garlanded, yet are called *diablots* and are armed with three-pronged forks or whips. Sometimes a man with a yoke of oxen ploughs a furrow round the dancing area, combining territorial defensiveness with an immemorially ancient incitement to Spring's fecundity.

Mompou may well have witnessed such a ceremony. The first of these two *gitanes* is marked 'très plaintif', and sounds it. Compared with the jollier gypsies that conclude *Impresiones Intimas*, these are primeval, recalling – even on an equal tempered piano – the 'deep song' of the *siguiriya gitana* and the

Mompou's 'Ludi Puerorum'

playera or 'weeping poem', wherein musical inflexions of the gypsy mell with Moorish cantillation and with memories of Byzantine liturgy. Mysteriously, Mompou's piano manages to evoke the latent orientalism of *cante jondo,* even to suggest microtonal alterations in the blues-like gapped scales. The exiguousness of the notes may have something to do with this; the music is not engulfed in pianistic luxuriance, so that one imagines one hears the vocalized Ay or Ah that warms up the feeling and cascades into quasi-microtonal undulations around a single pitch. In the first *gitane* the texture of flowing quavers is somewhat angular, with harshly secundal dissonances piercing the dorian C minor. The song fades in age-old melancholy through sighing augmented fifths, dominant ninth, and piled up fourths, perfect and tritonal. Mompou marks the passage *suppliant,* and its texture relates the gypsies to the *vieux cheval* rather than to the bustling humans of the previous pieces. An empty fifth C to G underpins this opening paragraph in timeless immobility, despite the rather painful texture: which grows more aggressive in the answering clause, *vif et agaçant,* in parallel fourths over a drone A flat – really an unresolved appoggiatura to the dominant G. The gypsies' slightly frantic energy is not, however, long-lived but peters out in dissonant four-part writing that ceases on an unresolved dissonance, to which Mompou appends a question mark; (we recall the children's 'interrogations' on the beach, in the *jeux* of *Scènes d'Enfants*). The passage is repeated *plus doucement,* this time to die of inanition in chromatic part-writing on a chord marked *sans espoir!*':

The dominant-tonic pedal is still there, a subterranean murmur. The da capo of the first section sounds in context yet more

Le Jardin Retrouvé

forlorn, the expiring cadence being *plus triste pour la dernière fois*.

The second *gitane* is less desperate but no happier. The rhythm is *inquiet* in a lurching 6 8 over guitar-plucked pedal notes that sound harsh and stringy rather than plangent. The pedal is on G and the modality phrygian. The middle section, if more lyrical, is wild, with Moorish-flamenco chromatic arabesques, stabbed by sudden outbursts of fury and *mauvaise humeur*:

Needing few notes to flesh out their scraggy bodies, these gypsies are uncomfortable characters whose modality distinguishes them from the plumper diatonic major of real kiddies: or if they are child-like in their instinctive natures, they remind us that children embrace nightmares along with dreams, truth being indivisible. The da capo is strict. As coda an A-E flat tritone, telescoped with the fifth G to D, remains suspended in mid air, so that the gypsy's anger, like his grief, seems timeless and placeless, relevant to us all.

If Mompou's gypsy is a hurt (but angry) child, companion to the hurt (but passive) beast of the first piece, so is the little blind girl portrayed in *La cuegeta*. At first she is whimpering (*péniblement*, like the horse!) a folk lament or plainchant-like begging-song in octave-doubled monody on D flat, though the tonality is basically G flat. Halfway through, her chant acquires an extra F flat, changing the mode to mixolydian as the lament whines in darker obsessiveness. The line doesn't become harmonic even when the tune is repeated in organum-like concords, high in register, with a drone accompaniment clinking in metallically semitonic dissonance, since the effect is

Mompou's 'Ludi Puerorum'

percussive: she seems to be bolstering her wail on a wheezy hurdygurdy:

The declining cadence through an augmented fifth is heart-rending. And although the final piece, *L'homme à l'Ariston*, is cheerful street music, melodically naif over an unchanging E flat pedal, its middle section is marked *gémissant et désaccordé*, and is so because the guitar player's rudimentary tonic, dominant and subdominant chords overlap in the seductive habanera rhythm. As a whole *Suburbis* touchingly and distinctively evokes the poetry of everyday reality: the pathos of the disparity between the things we do out there in the world, and what we esentially are in our once unfallen hearts.

The pieces discussed in this chapter reanimate the sung and danced games of children, creating a young adult's *recherche du temps perdu*. Children's games and runes are also the theme of a set of songs Mompou composed in 1926, and to which he added a second set in 1943, when he had attained the age of fifty. The Catalan or French words of these *Comptines* are either traditional or Mompou's own; often nonsensical, they are for and even by children rather than 'about' them, and to a degree this might be said of the music. The first number of the first set, *D'alt d'un cotxe*, has a tune restricted to the fourth between E and A. Simply symmetrical, it could be a real child's rune; and is accompanied by a primitive falling fourth and echoing major second, F and G above C, which is the tonic of the piano part, though the voice is ambiguously diatonic C major or phrygian E minor. Significantly, the style is identical with some of the piano *Charmes,* though those pieces are not specifically related to childhood. That the *ludus puerorum* is partly a *recherche* is hinted when a little coda, *très retenu,* flattens the falling scale

Le Jardin Retrouvé

and ends with an unresolved dissonance of a C minor triad with added second and sixth, *lointain*. Even in this genuine child's rune, which is as close to Satie's childhood music as Mompou comes, there's a tinge of nostalgia: as there is too at the end of the delightful *Margot la pie*, the vocal line contained within the fifth A to E, the piano part doubling the voice at the octave with its left hand, while enunciating Scotch snaps with its right. Again a fade-out adds a clinking E flat to an A minor triad with flat seventh. The third number is a danced game, the tune pentatonic, the accompaniment in ionian G major, with snappy repeated notes, parallel fourths and a drone bass.

But the most typical of the *Comptines*, and the most beautiful, is the first of the second set, *Aserrín, aserrán*, another nonsense song this time in march rhythm. The duple-metred tune veers between aeolian and dorian on G, the first half restricted to a fifth, expanding into the upper octave for its second half. The accompaniment is built mostly from Mompou's familiar fourths both perfect and tritonal; as we'll see, there are parallels with Mompou's folk dance pieces, and subtler ones with the quicker, or at least less slow, pieces from *Música Callada*. The second song in this set has a French text, and is even simpler, evoking its 'petite fille de Paris' first in monodic pentatonic incantation (we recall *La cuegeta* from *Suburbis*), then in gently swaying harmony teetering between mixolydian and dorian G. There are white note sevenths and ninths in the middle, though the song stops with the original pentatonic monody, unchanged. This sounds childish yet also very ancient: whereas the final *Comptine*, *Pito, pito, colorito*, is a game-song again in duple time, with a street jingle in clear diatonic A major, traditionally a key of youth and innocence. Grace notes tinkle in the piano part like tiny bells. Only a fleeting hint of F sharp minor disturbs the music's eternal present.

So far, we have considered those aspects of Mompou's music which spring from 'pre-historic' roots in spells and incantations; complementarily, we've examined works directly stem-

Mompou's 'Ludi Puerorum'

ming from the games of children, with whom primitive rites still subsist, even in the modern world. The nearest grown men and women come to this childhood magical-communal consciousness is in an agrarian peasant society such as still survives in Spain, and especially in Catalonia, though Mompou was not himself born into such a society. In the next chapter we turn to the music of Mompou moulded by his awareness of such *cançó i dansa*. As prelude, we must ask how the term 'folk music' may be most usefully delineated.

V

Mompou as Peasant Plus

> The proof of a poet is that his country absorbs him as he absorbs it.
>
> WALT WHITMAN
>
> We dance for pleasure and for the good of the City.
>
> Saying of the Zuni Indians

IN a sense all music is folk music: 'leastways, I never heard of no horse making it', as the great Louis Armstrong remarked of his own improvised com-position. None the less, the term 'folk music' is useful in defining an area of creation somewhere between primitive peoples' 'music of necessity' and the art song which is a product of 'Western' consciousness. So-called primitive man is not, in his song and dance, concerned with personal expression; on the contrary, far from seeking to assert his identity, he looks for *identification* with the tribe, subsuming individual will into collective consciousness. His repetitive, monophonic or heterophonic melodic figures conceive form as circular, without beginning, middle or end, fostering habituation to the world he lives in. Even when he recounts epic sagas of his race his approach is a-historical, oblivious of temporal progression. He cultivates, as do children who emulate him in their singing games, an eternal Now – what Geza Roheim has called 'the paradise of archetypes and repetition.'

At the further extreme the art song – the kind with which we, of course, are most familiar – has linear rather circular identity. It exists in time, having beginning, middle and end, since it is concerned with growth and change, and attempts to 'deal with' rather than to resist or evade them. The basic technical manifestation of this is that art songs are usually harmonic rather than purely melodic in structure. Harmony, being the simultaneous sounding of two or more tones, is of its nature dualistic, as monody, of its nature, is not. Dualism implies opposition and potential conflict: which seeks resolution in what came to be known as 'functional' tonality.

Folk song is a halfway house between these extremes, and is so both musically and anthropologically. Made by people living in relatively simple, self-enclosed agrarian societies which have contact with 'civilized' traditions, folk music may *begin,* like the savages' music, either with body-action incarnate in incremental repetition, as in work-songs or lullabies; or with syllabic incantation, as in epic ballads or funerary laments; or with a mixture of both. It moves, however, towards *song* which, though suspicious of temporality in a near-unchanging world, may have linear contour and continuity, and possibly some sense of progression: the qualities we define as melody. In this evolution there's give and take between communal and individual consciousness: as is reflected in the status of the 'folk' composer, who tends to be anonymous, or to become so. In a dark backward and abysm of time Some One invented a song: which others sing and (very gradually) modify to meet (very slowly) changing needs. In this way the song becomes at once personalized and collective. Not surprisingly its techniques, being linear if non-harmonic, may have much in common with art song: balance of phrases, gradation of intervals, variety (rather than mere repetition) of rhythmic pattern. Gradually, it leaves behind the per-form-ance techniques of primitive musics. Compromise with art techniques naturally increases as rural folk overlap with urban pop musics, as happens even in once remote areas, given the ubiquity of radio and television.

In using 'real' folk melodies, or in inventing tunes that might be mistaken for such, Mompou does not claim that he is a folk musician. He is an art composer of refinement, who finds in the folk songs and dances of his race an aspect of his own identity. He 'absorbs', to use Whitman's word, the country that made

Le Jardin Retrouvé

him, in a way that was possible for him in Catalonia, as it wasn't for Holst and Vaughan Williams in industrial Britain. Yet Mompou is not a nationalistic composer, as were Bartók and Janáček who, living in ethnically wilder Hungary and Moravia, found in their folk musics material for a radical reassessment of European tradition. Comparatively, Mompou was a Parisian sophisticate who found in his country's music a means of fostering his dreams of childhood and youth. In so far as his folk-style pieces make the past present, they accord with his rudimentary magic musics, for as Goethe put it, 'a conception of the past and present as being one ... infuses a *spectral* element into the present'. Over more than half a century Mompou composed piano pieces under the title of *Cançó i dansa*, usually taking the tunes and rhythms from the folk, sometimes making up his own tunes so similar that they can hardly be differentiated from the real thing. The Song, followed by the Dance, effects a contrast, in Mompou's words, between 'a slow melodious movement and a lively rhythmical one', the two being sometimes related, sometimes not. Between 1918 and the present day the formula has remained consistent.

With the possible exception of *Jeunes filles au jardin*, *Cançó i dansa* no. 1 (1921) is the best known of all Mompou's piano pieces: partly perhaps because it was the first of the series to be published, but more because the tune, especially that of the song, is so appealing. The melody arches up the scale from fifth to tonic, falls through a fourth, flattens the seventh, and descends to the third, notated in a ripe F sharp major. But the melody is supported by a drone fifth in the bass, harmonized with a triad with sharp third and flat seventh; the poignancy comes from the pervasive false relations, comparable with those of the black blues, and springing from a similar equivocation between melodic modality and harmonic diatonicism:

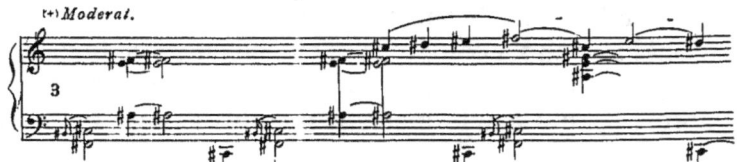

Mompou as Peasant Plus

Though the harmony is rich, it is static, with occasional chromatic passing notes and added notes, sometimes percussively non-harmonic, hinting at darker declivities. The Dance stays triple rhythmed and is thematically related to the Song, though their sources are distinct, the song being a Catalan love song, *La filla del Carmesi*, the dance a courtship rite called *bal de castelltercol*. The dance, being action music, gains momentum from its lilting dotted rhythm, but is still pervaded by a swaying ostinato around the fifth. Again harmony, though non-developing, exists, as in the Negro blues; indeed Mompou's harmony functions similarly, in 'personalizing' folk lament. In the dance the added notes are not so much dreamy as acid: as is evident even in the C natural in the first bar, in what looks like a dominant seventh of G over the F sharp ostinato. Later — especially in the passage marked *dins la boira* — added dissonances in small notes impart a metallic glint to the melody. Like the harmony, this is paradoxical, for the percussive sonority naturalistically imitates the 'ungrammatical' sounds of a peasant band, yet does so with a delicate artifice that distances the composer from Old Catalonia. The effect is very different from the rudely percussive peasantries in Bartók.

But there is a parallel with Chopin, especially the Chopin of the mazurkas wherein a highly sophisticated artist — also exiled in Paris — sought renewal in recollections of the peasant music he'd heard in his Polish childhood. The folk element in Chopin's 'Polish' pieces encourages a sinewy linearity and a partiality for the tritone-infested lydian mode; while his richly chromatic harmony imbues peasant spontaneity with a dreamy nostalgia for a mythology he 'cannot inherit'. Mompou, in his folk song and dance pieces, exhibits the same nostalgia by comparable technical means. Temperamentally, however, Catalan Mompou is closer than Polish Chopin to the child in Eden: which makes him a more single-minded but also a much more limited artist. This explains the difference that complements the likeness between the two composers' unresolved dissonances and passing notes. Chopin's harmony is sensuously enveloping; he

Le Jardin Retrouvé

enjoys his nostalgia as an adult. Mompou is usually less luxuriant, more bitter-sweet, even acerbic. The clashes and scrunches are sharp or (to use one of Mompou's favourite words) *clair*, even the dreamy added notes being precisely spaced. In this Mompou's harmony resembles that of Albéniz in *Iberia*, perhaps the greatest Spanish music since Spain's heroic ages in the Middle Ages and Renaissance. At first the parallel seems improbable, for Mompou's textures are transparent, whereas Albéniz's are dense. Even so, Albéniz's harmonic pulse is immensely slow: all the (long) pieces in *Iberia* are built, like Mompou's (short) pieces, over drones or folk-pedals, and only the harmonic passage-work is complex, adding guitar-like bite to the rhythmic momentum. Mompou uses much the same acid dissonances, only their articulation is slowed down. We're invited to savour them, in open-eyed and open-eared *wonderment*. This may be why his sophistication, unlike that of Albéniz or Chopin, paradoxically preserves the simplicity of a peasant, who may have the emotional integrity of a child.

Despite the erotic implications of this first Dansa, the music is profoundly Catalan in the sense defined in the preludial chapter, for it never relinquishes a hieratic solemnity. This quality is found no less in *Cançó i dansa* no. 2, which actually predates no. 1, having been composed in 1918. The popular tune on which it is based is called *Senyora Isabel*, and Mompou underlines its quasi-liturgical flavour with a deeply reverberating, gong-like G. The incantatorily repeated notes of the tune are doubled at the tenth, and haloed with undulating semiquavers that bump dissonantly into the pedal notes. The modality is aeolian G, but the sixth and seventh are sometimes sharpened in false relation. In its final clause the tune flows into triplets, with an effect ethereal in its freedom, yet also seductive in suggesting a physical gesture or caress. The dance is indeed *molt amable*, in straight ionian G major, with a gently arpeggiated tune over a wide-spaced drone. A chromatic alto part shades the texture more sensuously, prompting momentary modulations to dominant and relative in the second eight-bar clause. The tune even has a climax when the expansion of its upward leaping sixth to a seventh creates a piquant chord of the thirteenth which resolves, in a softly sighing augmented fifth, back to the clear tonic major.

These two pieces remain fairly close to folk sources. No. 3's *Cançó* is based on a Catalan Christmas song about the Virgin Mary; liturgical elements may be inherent in its folkiness, and in any case Mompou's handling of the exquisite arching melody in dotted triple rhythm is highly sophisticated. The melody is harmonized in sensuously spaced chromatics that trace inner voices:

A faint echo of jazz pianism, such as we noted in *Jeunes filles au jardin*, hints at a cocktail lounge within Mompou's rural landscape, underlining his dreamy nostalgia. But in this instance nostalgia is soon effaced, since the dance reasserts its folk origins unmistakably, even though it is an original tune. Here is the heart of the Catalan national dance, the sardana; the melody, restricted in compass to a sixth, is in mixolydian G, and is accompanied, *joyeusement*, by a bouncing dominant ostinato in 6 8. The harmony, if that's the right word, consists of percussive dissonances of unresolved fourths, E flat to A flat, 'standing for' D to G. The sonority, like that of a real sardana band, is harsh, and becomes more so when the tune returns after an eight-bar answering clause over a pedal A, with serpentine chromatics in the tenor and fours against threes in the top line:

Le Jardin Retrouvé

In the final clause tonality clears to ionian G major, and something like a climax is effected in a tipsy hemiola rhythm of 3 4 within 6 8.

The song of *Cançó i dansa* 4 (1928) is among the most beautiful in the series, though Mompou doesn't identify it. He does, however, print it on a separate stave, in order to distinguish the 'folk's' melody from his embellishments of it. Its heart-easing quality lies in the way in which its rising fourth flows into stepwise movement, flowers into an open G major arpeggio, then pentatonically declines. The tune itself is pentatonic on G, though Mompou's harmonization is pervaded, *avec douceur*, with chromatic passing notes and sighing suspensions. One chromatic chord resolves, or fails to resolve, on to another, inducing wistful regret, perhaps for a lost mode of living: consider the last line's flowing from German sixth to 6 4 with added second and sixth, to a hint of E minor, to the final appoggiatura in G major:

The pristine folk tune and Mompou's harmonized version of it are different but equally valid phenomena: the original entails the 'wholeness' of agrarian man or woman, while the Mompou version contains his and our separation from that wholeness, finding solace in retrospection.

In the *dansa* nostalgia leads to reanimation, for it sounds like fête music blaring in the boisterous present; the tonality veers between mixolydian and ionian G, in a sturdy duple metre. Passing dissonances in the inner parts are abrasive, as distinct from the expressive dissonances in the *cançó*. The movement – which being a round dance can, like the sardana of no. 3, be

Mompou as Peasant Plus

quite long – changes tempo to a martial 4 4 for its first episode, which sheds the chromaticisms to become a village band. The second episode babbles whirlingly in 6 8, alternating a spread tonic triad with a spread dominant ninth chord of B flat. Though the tingling acidity is not harmonically progressive, it gives a harder edge to the repeat of the rondo. Furthermore, it makes the da capo of the *cançó* which serves as coda one of Mompou's most magical moments. Neither the lovely tune nor its chromatic harmonization is changed, yet, after the dance, the nostalgia is the more poignant. Mompou marks it *en souvenir*. The remembrance is not merely of the original music, but also of a way of life.

The *Promenade* episode in this dance is reminiscent of the notated music of a small town band as well as of a village sardana band: which reminds us that the term folk song is sometimes loosely used to describe any tune sung (not necessarily created) by relatively uneducated people. Even an art song may, whether for musical or for adventitious reasons, become vastly popular, relished by many people irrespective of class barriers, and may circuitously enter the folk song genre. This happened even with some of the ballet and opera dance-songs of Lully, state composer to the *Roi Soleil* of 17th century France: than whom no-one ever composed music more ostensibly for the hyper-privileged. The ease with which folk and art musics mutually infiltrate may be indicative of the vitality of a society; certainly the almost complete divorce between the genres typical of the early years of this century amounts to a sickness.

Mompou's fifth *Cançó i dansa* (1942) presents a different kind of infiltration between folk and art elements since the art music it is related to is not pop but liturgical. The *cançó* is marked *lento liturgico*, and the idiom harks back to the ecclesiastical traditions of Spain's Golden Age, as described in the preludial chapter. For Mompou, as for Cabezón in the 16th century, 'tradition' embraces folk and art conventions impartially; he sees or hears no barriers between them, since the music 'folk' make on village greens cannot be rigidly segregated from

Le Jardin Retrouvé

the music heard in church; for fairly simple folk the sacred and the profane are, or may be, indivisible. The song may be an original creation in a traditional mould, the noble melody, in aeolian C sharp moving to F sharp, being plainchant-like but more rhythmically shaped. It is in three real parts, all readily singable:

The dance shifts from this grave modality to a radiant E major, no longer wary of sharp sevenths, with dissonant passing notes tingling like little bells over an open fifth drone. The metre is a lilting 6 4, *senza rigore* though the dance is sturdily harmonized in four parts, generating energy from arpeggiated chords that often move against the pulse. The fourth and seventh founded harmony, in keeping with that of the *cançó,* is austere.

Tempo changes from duple to triple for a sixteen-bar middle section in pristine A major, the subdominant. Marked *'semplice cerimonioso'*, the music suggests an altar dance in a rustic church; there's a slight stress on the second beat, as in a sarabande. The first eight bars are again harmonized in four quasi-vocal parts, with chromatic passing notes that create an equilibrium between discreetly public ceremony and no less discreetly private expressivity. These eight bars are repeated with the harmonies not changed, but more richly spaced on the keyboard, so that the false relations between melody and harmony notes are a shade more emotive. The dance ends ebulliently, folk vigour dominating Renaissance sophistication.

Cançó i dansa no. 6 (1942) also looks beyond Catalonia, though not to liturgical tradition. The Song, in a dark E flat minor, evokes 'antique' Spain in a melancholic melody alternating triplets with flowing scales, usually sighing into double appoggiaturas. The scoring is ripely in four or five parts, and it's

Mompou as Peasant Plus

the independent part-writing that generates the most lacerating dissonances: as for instance in the approach to the dominant ninth before the resolution back into E flat minor; and in the intermittent cadences on chords of the thirteenth – passionate sobs absorbed into the melody's gravity:

The final cadence, with its upthrusting tenor part, gives a further twist to the knife, before release into the Dance, which is as merry as the Song is mournful. *Ritmado* in 6 8, the piece exploits the Latin ambiguity between 6 8 and 3 4, though there is little harmonic, as distinct from rhythmic, movement. Of the pieces in the sequence, this one most resembles Albéniz's *Iberia*, the scrunchy harmonies of which here become translucent. The second half, in particular, having modulated upwards to the dominant, rivals Albéniz in the corybantic ardour it attains, though Mompou needs far fewer notes:

The composer himself described the piece as 'Creole, with vigorous and sensual rhythm evoking the bizarre style of the Antilles'. African, Cuban and Brazilian overtones transmute an Old into a (Latin American) New World. The end is not, however, totally affirmative; an added second echoes through the final tonic triad.

The melody of *Cançó* 7 bears some resemblance to *Aqui dalt de la montanya*, a mountain dance-song from the Aragon-Catalonian border, though its initial rising arpeggio is modified to incorporate a sharp seventh which in the descent becomes a

Le Jardin Retrouvé

dominant seventh in A major. The change makes the innocent tune both more sophisticated and more haunting, the more so because each time the aspiring phrase recurs it is more chromatically harmonized and more richly spaced. The 'eternal present' of a folk song is thus metamorphosed into a melody with beginning, middle and end, and with a cleanly spaced climax before its final cadence. One can understand why this number was Poulenc's favourite among the Songs and Dances. Both the melody and the texture have an *allure* such as we may also recognize in Poulenc's own finest music; as with Poulenc and Chopin, the harmony fits the melody like a glove, so that we can hardly remember the tune apart from its setting.

The *Dansa* shifts from the song's 6 8 to 3 4. Though more peasant-like in gait, it has a dignity typical of Renaissance court dance also, remembering that class barriers were then less evident, musically, than they became later. Passing notes gently chromaticize diatonicism; the middle clause, beginning with the original motif of rising sixth in the subdominant, gives a slightly nervous twist, by way of suspended sevenths and 'altered' notes, to peasant virility. Sensibility has the last word: for after a da capo of the original tune more powerfully scored, the coda, *meno mosso*, extracts the tenderest pathos from the 'middle's' altered notes, presented in vestigial canon, *dolce e espress*. Here again is regret for 'a mythology he cannot inherit', or perhaps just for childhood's forgotten garden:

The *Cançó* of no. 8 (1946) is a dance as well as a song, in a hypnotic triple rhythm, with stress on the second beat. The melody, gravely aeolian on G, is as much liturgical as folk-like. While the accompanying figure suggests a muffled gong or drum, the melody aspires upwards from its solemnly repeated

Mompou as Peasant Plus

Gs, modulating flatwards by way of affecting and affectionate dominant thirteenths. The *Dansa* is closely related to the *cançó*, the theme of which it opens into a rising triad in the tonic major. There's a real modulation to B minor, and seventh chords accrue from the lucid part-writing. Dissonances point the contours of the tune, to climax in massive, organum-like chords. This time the music stays loud even when, in the coda, added notes hint at 'nostalgias of another life'. This dream is potent.

Cançó 9 (1948) is based on a modified version of a Catalan song about a young man, his mother, and a nightingale. The tune is plain ionian E flat major, scored mostly in four parts, in hymnic sonority. The effect of the resonant texture is calm, the melody's declining scale, in resonant parallel sixths, being balanced by a gentle aspiration. A 'middle' in the aeolian mode on G is probably Mompou's addition, which breaks off on a chord of the thirteenth; is extended by way of chromatic sequences into a real modulation to the dominant; and proceeds to an assuaging da capo of the first clause. The Dance too, in fast triple time, springs from repeated notes, but unwontedly moves through sequential modulations. A middle, in the lower mediant, C major, doesn't abandon the repeated notes but reverts to Mompou's *'primitif'* manner, with drone fifths and open fourths to replace the more traditional, even academic, harmony of the first section. The da capo of the E flat dance ends, however, with a fade-out: an E flat triad reiterated like bells, with the overtone of a sharp lydian fourth:

Cançó 10 (1953) relinquishes folk sources, for its melody is quoted direct from the Cantigas of Alfonso el Sabio. As we've seen, Mompou does not sharply differentiate between such

Le Jardin Retrouvé

'antique' art musics and those that belong to the folk; this *cançó*, written in his sixties, is remarkably similar to the 'plaints' that open his first piano work, composed when he was seventeen. Like its model, this music crosses the boundary between Catalan religious folk song and liturgical art; we'll later observe how indistinguishable is its idiom from that of the music Mompou has made for liturgical use. The song is consistently aeolian, scored in four real parts, all white note, without a single chromatic alteration and, therefore, no modulation. None the less it sounds as Mompou-like as did those early pieces, perhaps because the diaphanous part-writing doesn't obey Renaissance prescriptions as to harmonic resolution. Dissonances are left suspended, in thin air; hints of canon dissipate. The sound, all in the middle of the keyboard, is pure, chaste, oddly disembodied:

The dance, *amabile* in triple time, is still incorrigibly white note but mixolydian, harmonized at first in three transparently spaced parts, then in four. The sonority, full of tenths, is balm-dispensing; even the more dissonant part-writing in the refrain is amiably vocal in contour.

This dance is Mompou's own complement to King Alfonso's cantiga. Something similar happens in no. 11 (1961), which opens in monody that might be a cantiga, or even plainsong itself, but isn't. When the incantation is harmonized, the texture remains exiguous; and the two related sections of the Dance – one in a floating 6 8, the other more courtly – do not deny, in their secularity, the spirituality of the *cançó*, for they distil grace in both the religious and the social sense. This makes a transition to the twelfth *Cançó i dansa* (1962), in which the song is based on a well-known Catalan melody about a Lady of

Mompou as Peasant Plus

Aragon with a long mane of blond hair: a troubadour's Eternal Beloved, and a fairy princess in her tower. The dance is another Catalan tune, *La mala nova*, insidiously rotating on itself. Yet although the material comes from traditional sources – in the dance directly from the 'folk', in the song from somewhere between folk and troubadour monody – this is among the most personal, and mysterious, of Mompou's pieces. Textures are very thin, and the technique of 'altered' notes is carried further than in any of the previous numbers, so that its effect might be called illusory as well as dreamy. The music has affinities with the aphoristic, introverted pieces that comprise *Música Callada*, in some ways the apex of Mompou's music, to be discussed in the final chapter. The sensuousness of the harmony remains, but is purged in the exiguous linearity; dissonant tones frequently stand for their resolution. The coda is especially fascinating: a fade-out in which the texture is at first sharp, even stark, so that in contrast the diaphanous added notes in the final chord sound from beyond the horizon. 'Catalonia' has become synonymous with Mompou's private vision.

These Songs and Dances, though all fashioned to the same pattern, are not meant to be a suite, nor necessarily to be played in sequences; they rather represent the composer's response to his heritage at various points in his long life. One may perhaps detect a slight evolution over the years. The first four, written between 1918 and 1921, are close to their folk sources; numbers 5 to 8, written between 1942 and 1946, and still more nos. 9 to 12, spread over the years from 1948 to 1962, modify folk elements with elements derived from liturgical incantation and from European art musics. The last of this group links with the most 'inward' aspects of Mompou's late works, and this probably applies to two later pieces in the genre which I haven't been able to see.

In the context of his 'Catalan' pieces it is appropriate to discuss Mompou's song cycle, *Combat del somni* which, apart from the miraculous little *Neu*, must count as his finest vocal music. Though it does not draw on folk 'material', it is

Le Jardin Retrouvé

profoundly Catalan in feeling, and is beautifully conceived for the human voice. This is what one might expect from a man who respects human nature and doesn't attempt to storm heights or plumb depths. His vocal lines avoid extreme registers, shaping themselves around the words, or even around the semi-articulate cries or murmurs that human beings utter – much as, in the piano music, 'themes' may be gestures that people, especially children, make in living, walking, breathing, dancing. Basically, Mompou's medium is solo piano, played not by a virtuoso but by himself to himself, or by you and me to ourselves. When a voice participates, it should sound as though a friend has called in, unheralded, or even as though the piano itself has acquired the gift of tongues, so close is the rapport between singer and player. Despite the subtle artifice of Mompou's songs, a measure of the artlessness of the folk or child singer does not come amiss in performing them.

The three songs of *Combat del somni* are spaced out between 1942, 1946 and 1948; a fourth number, added in 1961, is unpublished and I've been unable to see it. Yet although the songs are spread over a number of years they all set verses of the Catalan poet José Janés, have related poetic themes, and sound as though they are a cycle. The first song, *Damunt de tu nomes les flors*, not unexpectedly gives a mystical interpretation to sexual love. The woman seems to be dead, her body besprent with flowers. Stripped from their branches, the flowers also are dead or dying; the poet, becoming a flower's sigh, longs to expire along with them and her, entering the night in which they may be one in eternity. This basic awareness of mortality doesn't find incarnation in Mompou's magically static vein, but in a melody as memorable as a real folk song, so many of which tell, in a dour life, of the inescapable facts of death and decay. The poem sounds, at least in English, preciously *fin de siècle:* the music, however, is earthy in its melancholy, consoling an ageless grief as it flows, in a regular duple rhythm, in the aeolian mode on F, merging into diatonic F minor. Like a real folk song, the melody is in middle register, mostly by step or minor thirds,

Mompou as Peasant Plus

with an expansion to fourth or fifth in the approach to the cadences; conventionally, it covers eight plus eight bars. The piano part sounds nearly as spontaneous as the vocal line, for its quaver arpeggios suggest a guitar played, in immediate response to the words, by the singer himself. There are no dreamy or nostalgic added notes, for momently this grief is impersonal, the real right thing.

After a double bar, however, there's an answering clause for piano solo. Although this doesn't sunder the song's spontaneity, it intensifies it with chromatic sequences and modulations to E flat, B flat and A flat minors before returning, by way of a plangent dominant ninth of C minor, to the original F. The dense texture of this episode is created by the linear movement of inner parts, as so often happens in Mompou's folk song settings. It's as though the piano interlude is the composer's private commentary on the (sung) public lament, which is the folk's as well as his. And the lament survives intact for the second stanza which strophically repeats the first, as is normal in the unchanging peasant world. This time, however, the voice joins in the second, modulatory strain, for 'peasant' consciousness and 'artistic' sensibility have become inseparable. This is why Mompou can append a coda for piano solo, ending with an assuaging *tierce de Picardie:*

Le Jardin Retrouvé

At once a folk song and an art-song, *Damunt de tu* is lyrically memorable, even if it hasn't quite the singleness of mind and heart that makes *Neu* the composer's quintessential creation. *Neu* is spell, folk song and art-song simultaneously; in the later cycle Mompou separates the folk-art of the first number from the spell of the second, *Aquesta nit un mateix vent*, the words of which are overtly about a mystical union of souls and bodies through transparent air and illimitable sea: 'you are water, I am mirror'. Musically, the first section is literally entrancing: spell-binding by way of a figure in dotted rhythm reminiscent of that in Mompou's childish *Secreto*, lilting (*andante placido*) over a chord of fourths A to D to G, with a minor third on top. There is no harmonic progression, the chord oscillating between steps with A and G as bass. The secret of this hermetic song lies, however, in its voice part, which echoes the whole-tone implications of the piano part a tone lower. The rootless vocal line and harmony waver like seaweed in the tide, floating, appropriately enough, over unconscious depths:

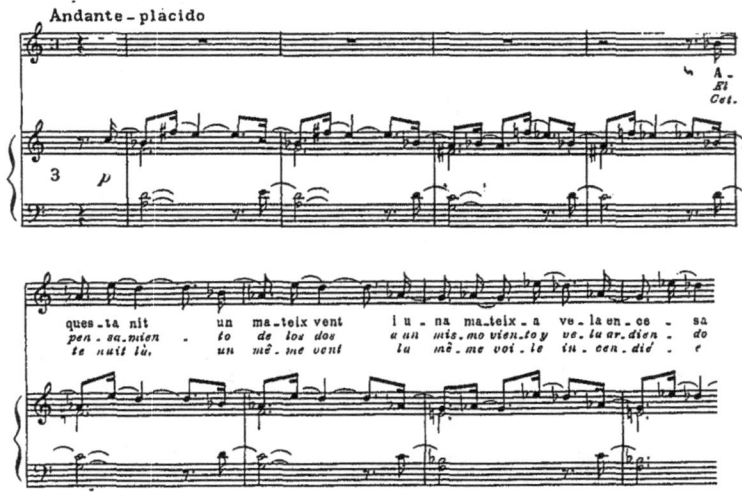

Chords of seventh, ninth and eleventh, usually in inversion, sink into flatter regions without establishing a key; the first section ends, *meno mosso*, with a repeated note incantation on the

Mompou as Peasant Plus

words 'El bas se'ns feia transparencia'. A da capo for the second stanza begins with a piano prelude in an A flat minorish region before returning to the original pitch. The refrain-incantation is repeated unchanged until, as coda, it caressingly resolves its harmonies into a smiling B flat major triad, widely spaced.

The words of the third song crown the cycle's erotic mysticism. The woman is not 'the blue image of a *human* dream' nor even 'the wind held in space'. She has 'no limits', and can be neither addressed in words nor imprisoned in a landscape. Like the troubadour's Eternal Beloved, she is infinite and illimitable, and so not far from the sea, and God. We've noted that sleep and the sea are pervasive images of the unknowable throughout Mompou's music: as of course they usually are, though Mompou, as a composer of *recommencement,* presents them in more than usually rudimentary terms. Musically, *Jo et pressentia com la mar* returns, rather surprisingly, to the folky manner of the first number, the voice having a duple rhythmed melody with rune-like characteristics, based on stepwise movement around the absolute consonance of the fifth, while the piano ripples in guitar arpeggios. The melody opens in pentatonic F sharp, but a cunning modal alteration of C sharp to C natural prompts a middle section which emulates wavery water in spread chords of the ninth and in illusorily shifting sequences. The da capo is straight and the song ends – it almost has a climax – with the tune expanded, its noble simplicity pointed by a chord of the thirteenth, with pause mark. The piano plays a postlude of F sharp minor arpeggios, guitar-like. The song is satisfyingly consummatory, if less melodically memorable than the communal-personal first number, and less spell-binding than the second.

Two Spanish songs, settings of Juan Ramón Jiménez made in 1945–47, come roughly into this folk-style category. *Pastoral* is a simple love song which again sees personal experience against the antiquity of folk culture. Its beautiful F sharp-aeolian melody, with repeated notes alternating with fourths and fifths, has liturgical overtones, recalling the fifth *Cançó i dansa*. The

Le Jardin Retrouvé

piano part intersperses chordal textures, often with secundal dissonances, into quasi-vocal polyphony which again, as in the solemner Songs and Dances, creates from chromatic alteration a texture bitter-sweet, even at times painful:

The second number, *Llueve sobre el rio*, also a love song, begins in the balladic style of *Damunt de tu*, with a duple rhythmed melody oscillating around the fifth of the tonic B flat, and a swaying accompaniment suggesting physical gestures. The second strain, however, referring to love's anxieties, loses its folk-rooted stability, being harmonized in Mompou's 'hieratic' parallel dissonances. In this case they're metallic seventh chords, prophetic of the harsher sonorities of *Música Callada*. This music is more bitter than sweet; the end, on a low B flat rare in Mompou's vocal writing, sombrely asserts a B flat minor triad.

Another song, *Aureana do sil*, a setting of Ramón Cabanillas dating from 1951, deserves a mention appropriate to its two-page brevity, since its swaying 6 8 melody resembles the folk-like tunes among the songs commented on above, but the spaciously laid out piano part is far more sophisticated. The same altered chords recur with very different effect, since the opulent keyboard writing rounds off their edges. When the glowing ninths and elevenths mount, *molto rit*, to an impassioned climax, the unabashed romanticism recalls not only Chopin, but the Granados of *Goyescas;* one can even hear Bill Evans playing it with affection:

Mompou as Peasant Plus

This little song, though not vintage Mompou, therefore provides a transition from those aspects of his work that derive from spells, from children's games and from Old Catalonia, to those aspects wherein he contacts the modern world. In the next chapter we'll consider Mompou's relationships with 'Europe' and with 'Art'.

VI

Mompou and 'Europe', Adolescence and Art

'The child is father to the man'.
How can he be? The words are wild.
Suck any sense from that who can:
'The child is father to the man'.

No; what the poet did write ran
'The man is father to the child'.
'The child is father to the man!'
How can he be? The words are wild.

   GERARD MANLEY HOPKINS

MOMPOU'S charms, spells and festivities, his children's runes and games, are moments of being, music of an eternal present. The sequence of Songs and Dances are also festively ceremonial, but are rooted in a people's history, and so aware of past as well as present. Though they tend to be longer than the spells and games, they *go on* only because, if they were real folk songs and dances, people might be acting or dancing to them – and perhaps, in a more general sense, because agrarian communities are strong on survival. The structural principle, if it can be called such, of these longer pieces is that of variation – slight changes in or embellishments to a *single* theme; or of rondo or round dance – a *single* tune repeated unchanged any number of times, with each statement separated by an episode usually related to the main theme, but without developmental effect upon it. When Mompou composes music affiliated to European

Mompou and 'Europe', Adolescence and Art

art musics rather than to primitive incantation or folk song and dance, he not surprisingly uses brief, self-enclosed forms or forms which, if longer, are variations or rondo. Either way, his mentor is Chopin: who perhaps represents for Mompou the transition from childhood to adolescence, though of course Chopin himself grew from adolescence to a complex maturity. There's also some parallel between Mompou and the young Schumann, who composed for piano brief 'moments of sensation', often in waltz rhythm, and frequently strung together chains of small pieces on something approaching variation principle – as in the *Kinderscenen*, patently a Mompou theme. His finest large-scale works are more commonly a variation set, like the *Etudes symphoniques*, than a sonata.

A key early work among Mompou's 'arty' pieces is the *Trois Variations*, composed in 1921, very soon after he'd settled in Paris. The work lasts a mere four minutes; and the theme, were it barred, would amount to no more than four plus four bars of 2 2, presented monodically, on a single stave. It would be presumptuous to call it a melody; even the directive *Très simplement*, is unnecessary, for one could not imagine a more guileless child's rune. It rocks between F and the minor third above and moves up to the fourth; but the symmetrical answering clause faintly stains innocence with a descending *diminished* fourth! The little tune is played twice, and that's it; nor is the *tune* modified in the three variations.

At the end of the monodic theme it appears that the implicit tonic is mixolydian B flat. But the first variation, *Les soldats*, though it presents the tune at the original pitches an octave higher, is supported – rather than harmonized – with an E flat-B flat drone. Chromatic passing notes sink through the tenor register while offering no hint of harmonic progression. Only at the end does the gentle march rhythm suggest addition to, if not variation of, the tune itself, as a (toy?) trumpet tootles a military fanfare marked, however, with the familiar *lointain*. This dissolves into chromatic seventh chords, leaving the cornet to echo into silence:

Le Jardin Retrouvé

Clearly this is little-boy Mompou, whose variations are dedicated *'à mon père'*.

The second variation, *Courtoisie*, keeps the tune in the upper octave, still unaltered except for a lilting dotted movement in its *'très aimable'* valse. The theme had seemed to be monodically in modal B flat, the first variation in E flat. This second variation, without change to the pitch of the tune, is in D flat, with a resonantly spaced texture one might call Chopinesque, though its immediate ancestry is in the triple rhythmed dance of those *jeunes filles* in the paradisal garden of *Scènes d'enfants*. The girls are growing up into the adolescent social round in which courtesy — such gracefully waltzing movement, such elegant bowing without scraping! — is a *sine qua non*. Growth is latent in the mere fact that the second four bars, still with no change to the tune, sequentially modulate, by way of luscious suspensions and chords of the thirteenth, through G flat major, E flat minor and A flat major. It would be almost like the cocktail-lounge music hinted at in *Aureana do sil,* were it not still virginal in its sensuality:

But in the third variation, *Le crapaud*, the social world — whether that of the little boy who manipulates toy soldiers into a rudimentary game of adult life, or that of the *jeune fille* approaching, maybe, sexual as well as social intercourse — is abandoned. Far from proceeding from childhood through adolescence to adulthood, Mompou indeed effects a *'recommencement'*, once again facing Nature's ongoing, unchanging reality, independent of childhood games or adolescent dreams. The toad croaks *dans le silence de la nuit*. The tune, still in the top voice, still identical in pitch with its first statement, floats regardless of the up and down flowing arpeggios that telescope the tonic and dominant seventh of E flat minor – as, perhaps significantly, does the love-spell from *Charmes,* written in the same year. The modality, previously ambiguous, would seem to be established as E flat, with a side-step to D flat before the cadence at the end of the first statement. In the second and third repetitions of the unaltered tune the arpeggios delineate a counter-melody, tenderly hesitant because off-beat. As so often in Mompou, the music gradually runs down, reversing the clock's temporal process, tune and arpeggios dissolving into appoggiaturas that are both technically and emotionally quavery. The A to G sharp appoggiatura 'stands for' B double flat to A flat, but the enharmonic notation is justified since it betrays the *otherness* of the peeping creature, who looks off-key on the printed page, and sounds it, however grammatically explicable. Toad or bird, this creature is also the young Mompou: a boy-man who may have relinquished playing at soldiers and at teenage gallantries, but who, unsure whether growing up *is* progression, prefers to return to an 'unaccommodated' state. In the enveloping darkness he's like the shaman who becomes crying bird or squawking cat, ready to confront, or even to identify himself with, 'things that go bump in the night'. Despite or because of their rudimentariness, these variations are a very basic, and strangely moving, Mompou piece.

From time to time Mompou has composed short piano pieces which, in homage to Chopin's wondrous set in all the major and minor keys, he calls Prelude. The first set, dated 1928, is linked not so much with Mompou's magic and childhood pieces as with his apprentice-work, *Impresiones Intimas,* though the first number, headed *Romance,* also has affinities with his

Le Jardin Retrouvé

Catalan vein. The haunting melody – in a flowing 12 8 with hemiola cross rhythms – is melodically and rhythmically folk-like, while the G sharp minor and C sharp minor-major harmony is luxuriant. Like a Chopin mazurka, the piece is a personal gloss on communal experience, *dans le style romance* in the Renaissance sense, and possibly in the 19th century sense also. The second piece is, however, more like a *cançó i dansa*, with an incantatory introit, erupting in flamenco-like arabesques, breaking off in agitation, but leading into a white note hymn, *très simple* in three widely spaced parts. This prelude proves to be more episodic than a *cançó i dansa*, for the hymn leads into a new version of the incantation, over a low E pedal, with echoing bells in the treble. Gypsyish agitation spurts out again, the adjective being used metaphorically to suggest that the tune, though not a gypsy song, hints in its augmented and by implication microtonal intervals at gypsy waywardness and non-conformity. When the agitated motif is repeated with chromatic harmonies, the sound is ripe but *prickly*. This oddly episodic piece – one damn thing after another, again – equivocates between harsh reality and regretful dream. At the end the original *énergique* incantation echoes *un peu lointain* if *toujours clair*, as though on a distant shepherd's pipe. A rocking ostinato between D-G and F sharp-C sharp grumbles, *sourd*, beneath, but unsynchronized with, the piper's arabesques:

Mompou and 'Europe', Adolescence and Art

This Prelude is still relateable to Mompou's magical and Catalan veins; the third overtly suggests Chopin in lay-out and figuration, despite its Spanish 12 8 lilt. Basically in E flat major, the bass moves, for Mompou, expansively, while arpeggios create bitonal ambiguities by way of unresolved, or only partially resolved, appoggiaturas:

This music's sensuousness, like Chopin's, is romantically personal, even introspective: while the final prelude of the set is again a *cançó,* in triple rhythm and in four real parts veering between the lydian and aeolian modes. It recalls the quasi-Renaissance dances in *Impresiones Intimas,* and like them is content with a rudimentary ternary form. The slow middle, with weeping appoggiaturas, double dots and chromatics, makes personal response to the dance's communality. The tribe is not, however, bothered by the introspection, for the da capo of the dance is strict.

Preludes 5 and 6 – the first two of the second set – were written in 1930, soon after the first set. Preludes 8, 9 and 10 date from 1943 and 1944, while no. 7 was composed in 1951. As one might expect, given that they span a period of twenty years, these preludes are both backward and forward looking. No. 5 is an especially beautiful song-dance-song in the aeolian mode on D, beginning with an arching, triple rhythmed tune simply harmonized, though with a few (non-chromatic) dissonances. The bounding 'middle' moves in animated duple rhythm, with parallel sevenths over tonic and dominant pedals that suggest folk bagpipes and hurdygurdies. Only in the coda do dreamy added notes insinuate themselves, separating us from the peasant world. Whereas this prelude relates to Mompou's magical and folk manners, no. 6 is romantically introverted,

Le Jardin Retrouvé

like the first book's prelude in the same key, E flat. It is cunningly contrived for the left hand alone, which delineates inner voices within broken arpeggios, creating bitonal effects – like that *crapaud dans le silence de la nuit* – from irregularly resolved appoggiaturas.

Among preludes of later date nos. 8 and 9 relate to Chopinesque romanticism, but also look towards the bittersweet austerities of Mompou's 'late' style, as exemplified in *Música Callada*. Prelude 8, unbarred and without key signature, is marked *con lirico espressione*. Vestigially imitative 'points' gather energy from the original 'speaking' phrases in falling scales which, inverted, move through whole tone progressions and parallel dominant sevenths. The rhythmic freedom and the acidulated textures anticipate *Música Callada*, though the rich sequential harmonies and the (for Mompou) impassioned climax are more Chopinesque. Tonality presses cyclically sharpwards from D major to F sharp major, then luxuriously resolves back into D major, with luminous added seconds:

The lovely ninth Prelude is sensually languid, somewhere between folk lament and self-confession – as are many of Chopin's Polish pieces. The 6 8 melody undulates between seventh and ninth chords, sometimes major, sometimes minor, often enharmonically notated. In the 'middle' they burst into

Mompou and 'Europe', Adolescence and Art

wide-flung sequential ninths, the melody chanting in octaves. Having arrived at A flat minor, the music subsides to its original indeterminacy. Not until the seventh bar of the shortened da capo is the C sharp minor tonality established.

These two fine preludes are halfway between folk experience and the romantic's solitary heart; and one could say the same of the tenth, which oscillates between a chordally supported, dotted rhythmed processional theme in Mompou's *festiva* vein and a mysteriously enharmonic dialogue, with 'expressive' appoggiaturas. The remaining Prelude, no. 7, dating from seven years later than the others, is an odd man out, being subtitled *Palmier d'Etoiles*, and representing a Catalan festival in episodically impressionistic, rather than folky, style. A rampant display of fireworks is emulated by brokenly dissonant arpeggios, explosive chords of piled-up fourths, and even a stratospherically shooting scale. A folk lament, rocking through a sixth, winds (*molto tranquillo*) through the festivities, underlining the valediction within carni-val, which says farewell to the flesh not only because of Lent's advent, but also because all flesh is grass, and we must expire like the sputtering fireworks.

This piece is neither very good nor characteristic Mompou, though it is distinguishable from the routine descriptive piano pieces that surfaced in the wake of Debussy. Other piano works of Mompou's middle years fail fully to convince for similar reasons, notably the three *Paisajes,* grouped as a set though written respectively in 1942, 1946 and 1960. The best of them, *La fuente y la campa*, has a touching tune in pentatonic G minor, and evokes the mystical associations of fountains and of monastery bells. We are reminded that many Catalan songs to saints and the Virgin also function as prayers for rain and fertility; at Cervera a conventional Moors-against-Christians *morisca* celebrates too the carrying of water from the fountain-sanctuary of Sant Magi to be offered at every house, after an eight-hour climb, by a dancer representing the saint himself. Folk ritual echoes in the water images of *El lago* also, while the longest piece, *Carros de Galicia*, metamorphoses village cere-

Le Jardin Retrouvé

monies into the interior world of *Música Callada*. The mystical or religious aura of this bell-tolling piece may owe something to its regional association with Galicia, spiritual heart of Spain and home of the S. Alonso *cantigas*. Its motif of falling seventh, which may be a call to prayer, is significantly marked *très lointain*, however, and the music hasn't yet achieved the concision and 'inwardness' of *Música Callada*.

These post-impressionist pieces are peripheral to the 'European' tradition: to explore Mompou's relation to which we must return to his links with Chopin. A key work is the two *Dialogues* of 1923; for if the *Trois Variations* of two years earlier are the first work to reveal Mompou's interest in variation as a 'romantic' formal principle, the *Dialogues* are the first wherein he investigates a more spaciously Chopin-like keyboard idiom. No. 1 begins with a folk-plaint such as we're familiar with from *Impresiones Intimas* and from the various Songs and Dances. An aeolian tune with 'speaking' repeated notes is harmonized in white notes forming parallel 6 3 chords. The liturgical flavour vanishes when they're chromaticized in the seventh and eighth bars; and cease, *sans espoir*, on an unresolved, false related dissonance and a (written) question mark. We recall those hopeless gypsies in *Suburbis;* this passage seems likewise to say goodbye to an antique world we've grown out of. But the dialogue that follows asks more searching questions: a floating melody with gypsyish modal distortions (in a modified phrygian mode on E, with flat second and sharp fourth and sixth?) is accompanied by Chopinesque D minor arpeggios stretched to embrace B natural. At the end of this clause another question is asked, *plus suppliant*, in a falling scale; and is answered *plus décidé*, the repeated notes now agitated by chirruping thirds in grace notes. The undulating arpeggio embraces tonic *and* dominant of D major, sharpened – in a technical and an emotive sense – by the intrusion of A sharps and E sharps:

Mompou and 'Europe', Adolescence and Art

The arpeggio fades in major-minor ambiguity, while the melody hesitates on unresolved fourths.

These questions and responses, if not answers, remain indeterminate; perhaps they concern Mompou's and our futures, poised as we are between worlds. This applies no less to the second *Dialogue*, which again precipitates from wide-undulating arpeggios melodic 'gestures' that seem to imply human conversation. Pseudo-polyphony is generated by Chopin-like cross accents within the arpeggios. Prompted by Satie, Mompou tells the performer how to interpret the gestures – *expliquez, exaltez vous, donnez des excuses*. But the verbal gloss is redundant, so intimately does the music speak *dans la pensée*. The phrase suggests how Mompou's music is ceasing to be magic, spell or game and is turning inwards: though its therapeutic efficacy remains – adapted to the solitariness modern man lives in, as compared with the members of a tribe of savages or children. The end of this beautiful and original piece is a mere cessation; the G minor triad has added notes – D, E and A – that could be major.

The piano style of the *Dialogues* prepares the ground for Mompou's one attempt at a large-scale piano work, modestly taking its place in European tradition. His *Variations sur un thème de Chopin* occupied him for nearly twenty years, being

Le Jardin Retrouvé

started in 1938 but not finished, or at least published, until 1957. Taking as starting-point Chopin's two-line A major prelude from opus 28, Mompou makes a work lasting more than twenty minutes. Even so, this doesn't modify his predilection for small forms since these variations, like those of the young Schumann, are 'moments' which neither receive nor need development. At first he quotes Chopin's idealized prelude-valse-mazurka (at once Polish and Parisian) in its sixteen-bar simplicity. In Variation 1 he reveals its mazurka-potential, embellishing it with double and triple chromatic appoggiaturas, all of which are at least implicit in Chopin's original. Dissonant passing notes ring through the lushly spaced chords; private expressivity, as with Chopin, transmutes the folk source. The second variation works similarly, though there is now a tang of Spanish acerbity. The pulse has changed to a gracious 6 8; the appogiaturas tingle in false relation. Again one can hear Bill Evans negotiating the last two bars with exactly the right mingle of swing and *tendresse*.

Variation 3, for the left hand alone, moves to the subdominant, and resembles the left-handed Prelude in creating pseudo-polyphony from interlacing arpeggios. The appoggiaturas, in false relation, induce pathos, with an undertow of Spanish lament: so we're prepared for the fourth variation to move into genuine Mompou territory, with quasi-canonic modal polyphony in the flat submediant, pastoral F major. The tempo is a gentle 2 4. Chromaticized expressivity in the cadences modifies the Catalan manner, as does a middle section in the more austerely linear idiom of *Música Callada*. Nostalgia becomes overt in the dominant thirteenth before the last statement of the tune, and in the meltingly chromaticized final cadence:

Mompou and 'Europe', Adolescence and Art

This may be why, in the fifth variation, Mompou compensatorily turns Chopin's putative mazurka into a real one, brusque in rhythm, harsh rather than languid in appoggiaturaed dissonance. Once again the wide spread chords in the approach to the cadences imbue folk vigour with dreaminess, as though it is something looked *back* to, however ardently. And the sixth variation is highly hermetic music which begins as folk lament recurrently exploding into dissonant false relations; transforms its incantation into dotted rhythm figures derived from the previous mazurka-variation; dissolves in whole-tone chords; blows up still more violently in the false related dissonances; and fades on the open fifth:

The variation is so close to *Música Callada* in style that one suspects it may be a late addition to the variation-set. None the less, Chopin's theme is not lost sight or sound of.

This variation has no definite tonality though it vacillates, except in its whole-tone middle section, around a dorian G. For variation 7 Mompou returns to A major and to Chopin, producing a miniature Chopin *Etude* moving, in rapid 3 8, through volatile chromatic harmonies at first over a tonic pedal, then over a bass moving very slowly. There's a modest hint here of the joyous liberation Chopin achieves through the keyboard's virtuosic response to his fluttering fingers, nerves and senses. But this extroversion is balanced by the introversion of variation 8, also Chopinesque, but in the self-communing mood of the wondrous E minor Prelude. The melody is absorbed into softly pulsing quaver chords in F major, the flat submediant: which may link the personal expressivity of this variation to the folk poetry of the fourth variation in the same

Le Jardin Retrouvé

key. Passing dissonances glow mellifluously, while an ostinato F, stressing the second beat of the swaying 3 4, rings through the harmonies like a distant horn. The combination of harmonic sensuality with lyric tune is here closer to Poulenc than to Chopin, though the Polish master was the wellspring in both cases.

This reference to Poulenc bears on what happens in the rest of the work: for in variation 9 Mompou returns to the original A major and metamorphoses a Polish mazurka into a French valse. The sweet harmonies of Chopin's original expand into salon-like opulence; in the final statement the keyboard spacing suggests a sublimated cocktail lounge, in which a cabaret pianist is improvising. Such effects are familiar in Poulenc's *café-chantant* vein, sometimes parodistically, as in the song *Hôtel*, sometimes as unselfconscious hedonism. Mompou embraces the mode without surrendering his identity, for the answering eight – in the aeolian mode on F sharp, with dominant and tonic drones – sounds simultaneously French and Catalan.

Ambiguity, even duality, between folk experience and a modern social word pervades the rest of the work. Variation 10, called *Evocation*, evokes 'old' Catalonia, being still in aeolian F sharp, though riddled with sighing appoggiaturas and pungent false relations, comparable with the fifth *Cançó* and the song *Pastoral* from the Jiménez settings. The middle is a hymnic dance in A major, in Mompou's folk-Renaissance, peasant-courtly, vein: as far from Chopin's tune as is a Catalan village from a Parisian salon. But in variation 11 Mompou leaps from past to present, beginning with arpeggiated chords wherein the melody, as in the *Dialogues*, is both rhythmically and harmonically veiled, but exploding into surprisingly unbuttoned passion, with sequential sevenths and ninths recalling the luxuriance of Granados rather than Albéniz's darker intensity. What Jelly Roll Morton called 'the Spanish tinge' endemic in jazz is also latent if not patent:

Mompou and 'Europe', Adolescence and Art

The luxuriant piano texture suggests not so much Bill Evans as blind, black Art Tatum who, although belonging to an earlier generation than Evans, was scarcely launched on his career when Mompou's Variations were written. None the less, there's an intuitive affinity between Mompou's fusion of (rhythmic and melodic) passion with (chromatic harmonic) dream and Tatum's compromise between African blackness and American whiteness. We noted another instance in the little song *Aureana do sil*.

But Mompou's homage to Chopin doesn't end in this Catalan-Parisian-Polish-American cocktail lounge, for this variation, tremulously quivering out on an F sharp minor triad with added notes, bounds into a *Galope* over droning fifths on A or F sharp, with semiquaver thirds fluttering Chopin's double appoggiaturas into major-minor ambiguity. Far from being mindlessly efferverscent, like an Offenbach galop or Poulenc's imitation of one, this music is rough in texture, grumpy in register. Jazzy sequential sevenths and ninths drive the galop towards a *molto cantabile* version of Chopin's tune, twice as slow, in what jazzmen call double time. The melody is accompanied by throbbing quaver chords as sumptuous as Poulenc's, and hardly distinguishable from them. The big, sometimes whole-tone, chords are grandly scored – fleetingly, we may think of Rachmaninov – to support the soaring tune; for a brief while this must be easily the loudest music Mompou ever wrote:

Le Jardin Retrouvé

It's as though 'timid' Mompou, with his ancient Catalan heritage, is momently fulfilled in Poulenc-like social bonhomie, here and now in the urban social world. But it cannot last. The melody returns to the non-melodic galop and the variation concludes with a deliberately perfunctory stretto and three pawky tonic triads – blatantly 'final', as Mompou scarcely ever is.

He isn't really being final, however, since this Galop is followed by an *Epílogo*, which returns to Chopin's Prelude and its triple rhythm, slower, with the chromatic appoggiaturas and passing notes more tender because more widely spaced. Here the texture is too rarefied to recall Art Tatum, though another jazz pianist, the whitely elegant Bill Evans several times referred to, used linearly spaced chromatics to comparable effect. Pathos is enhanced as the appoggiaturas, each 'resolving' on to an acuter dissonance, give a sharper edge to the sensuality:

Mompou's tender heart is still solitary, despite his transient approach to Society and to the Good Life which, a perennial child, he proves content, or strong enough, to eschew. The little boy who, for a moment, almost grasped those goodies in the sweetshop window has not, after all, gobbled them up.

VII

Mompou, the Church, and 'La Soledad Sonora'

> Our first parents still danced among the angelic powers. But the beginning of sin made an end to the sweet sounds of that chorus. Since then, man has been deprived of this communion with the angels and, since the Fall, must sweat and arduously do battle with and conquer the spirit that, thanks to sin, now weighs upon him. But the spoils of victory will be these: that which was lost in the original defeat will once more be his to enjoy, and once more he will take part in that divine chorus.
>
> GREGORY OF NYSSA: *Homiliae 6.*

> Christianity incontestably proves to be the religion of 'fallen men': and this to the extent to which modern man is irremediably identified with history and progress, and to which history and progress are a fall, both implying the final abandonment of the paradise of archetypes and repetition.
>
> GEZA ROHEIM: *The Myth of the Eternal Return*

WE have observed Mompou's music veering between primitive spells, games and incantations and the expressive demands of Art, in the European sense. His affiliations with art were mainly with early romanticism; but there is another aspect of 'Europe' which, although a central artistic tradition, is also close to his folk origins. This is the Catholic Church which, especially in 'backward' Spain, has remained unchanged, if not moribund, for hundreds of years. The only music Mompou has composed other than his small pieces and songs is for the liturgy of his

Le Jardin Retrouvé

Church. In style this music is hardly distinguishable from the religious vein we have commented on in his Songs and Dances and in the *Impresiones Intimas*. These quasi-religious pieces are, we noted, usually written in three or four real parts which could be sung. Some of them use melodies from the Cantigas of Alfonso X, two of which Mompou arranged in four-part vocal polyphony in 1953. In the same idiom are a few pieces written for liturgical use, to Latin texts: of which the best known and most beautiful is an *Ave Maria* for SATBB, dated 1958. Each line moves, plainsong-like, by step or by 'vocal' intervals of minor third, fourth or fifth, producing plain diatonic concords with a minimum of chromatic alteration. The modality is sometimes aeolian, sometimes dorian, though the melodic contours are often pentatonic. Harmonically, the diatonic texture is pervaded by fourths, fifths and sevenths as much as by triads, sounding like a cross between Medieval and Renaissance vocal idiom, as is apposite to Mompou's view of music and the world. There is no modulation, though modality oscillates between E, A and B, always gravitating back to E. Except for a briefly lilting interlude in 6 8, the music is consistently in duple time, at about the speed of the pulse, and the texture is constantly homophonic.

This differs from early Renaissance liturgical music only because its voices do not always behave grammatically, in accord with Palestrinian prescription: parallel sevenths, as well as fourths and fifths, are frequent, and dissonances, usually mild major seconds, may be left unresolved. The serenity of the music is at once spiritual in the ametrical, Palestrina-like continuity of the lines, and sensual in the smiling euphony the parts create together. Not for nothing is the motet a hymn to the Virgin Mary, whose femininity had soothed and succoured medieval peasants, as it does 'child-like' Mompou in our barbarous present. The serenity of the music, given the world we live in, is strangely affecting; only a man pure in heart could have made it. Even so, it is hardly surprising that the effect should be curiously disembodied; we may momentarily join Mompou in seeking a

Mompou, the Church, and 'La Soledad Sonora'

haven of quiet within his (Catalan village?) church, but cannot pretend that this is 'functional' music in the world at large. Why should it be? Mompou would no doubt retort that a near-private church is better than none.

But on one occasion the Church, a public institution, did prompt Mompou to create a large-scale work involving performers other than piano and voice. His *Impropreria* was commissioned in 1964 for the *Tercera Semana de Música Religiosa de Cuenca*, and sets its Latin text on the model of a dramatic oratorio rather than of liturgical music proper, though it was intended for ecclesiastical performance. It is scored for baritone solo, mixed chorus and a slightly modified classical orchestra of double woodwind, four horns, two trumpets, three trombones, tuba, strings and percussion, plus celesta and harp. It lasts nearly thirty minutes; yet it is not really a 'big' work since its structure is again episodic, a series of Moments rather than an evolution through time. This atemporal quality, appropriate to worship, is palpable in the orchestral prelude, which is brief and Satie-like in undulating between non-progressive concords, characteristically scored to resemble chime-like bells. The harmony is less chaste than Satie's; there's a touch of neo-Renaissance Poulenc, and even of early Messiaen.

The first vocal section, *Popule meus*, involves the folk – you and me – in the religious rite, being built on antiphony between the soloist as priest and the chorus as congregation. The baritone at first sings monodically, in modal incantation close to plainchant; the chorus moves homophonically, mostly in diatonic concords suggesting, as does Carl Orff in comparably Christian contexts, the child-like aspects of the worshipping medieval peasant. Since neither Mompou nor his congregation is in fact a medieval peasant, however, the soloist becomes an 'I', an individual consciousness, as well as God's representative; and in the *Hagios o Theos* (*Sancte Deus*) the choir too absorbs his personal expressivity, singing impassioned music springing from a theme undulating through a semitone, drooping through a fifth. At 'Quia eduxi te' the orchestra responds in brief

Le Jardin Retrouvé

ferocity. If Mompou's sonorities here recall the Stravinsky of *Symphony of Psalms*, they lack the severity of that great work, being closer to the mellower timbres of Poulenc's Stravinskian imitations – in, for instance, his *Gloria*. When, in faster orchestral interludes, Mompou exploits sharp, edgy sonorities, he relates them to Catalan folk bands and processional music, so that their public stance is simpler, even naiver, than that of comparable passages in Stravinsky.

Although the work is episodic, its sections increase in length and substance, so that the *Ego te pavi* provides a culmination, if not climax, to the whole. The quasi-liturgical theme is based on a scale declining through a fourth in dotted rhythm, rounded off by a godly falling fifth. This melody is deployed broadly, with an effect similar to that of the larger church works of Poulenc. The only Mompou music it resembles is the later variations from his only other large-scale piece, the Chopin variations. Here, as there, the music does *go on*, and is the closest Mompou comes to making music about the relation between the self and the world it inhabits. The *Crucem tuam adoremus*, morever, after a briefly ferocious, peasant-style orchestral eruption (the 'acts of God' that afflict unknowing us?), resolves passion into quietude, as the soloist sings serenely *with* the choir. The work ends with modal oscillations – a murmur of prayer – similar to those with which it opened, for the liturgical cycle is perennial, as are the seasons of the year.

Although the *Impropreria* is an intermittently moving creation it does not persuade us that public statements are congenial to Mompou, whose liturgical music owes its lovely simplicity to his being, in a near obsolete sense, a man of faith. So it is not in a public statement that we find the heart of his religious experience which, for someone concerned with spiritual *recommencement*, must be the basis of *all* experience. Among his ecclesiastical pieces those that approach most nearly to that heart are significantly not strictly liturgical, but settings of Catholic mystical poets such as Pedro Masaveu. We may take as typical his setting of the pertinently titled *Vida interior* of 1966.

Mompou, the Church, and 'La Soledad Sonora'

Again it is scored for SATBB, the second bass — as in the *Ave Maria* — seldom having an independent part but rather doubling the first bass or tenor, thereby stabilizing the homophony. Though the parts move mostly stepwise, or by third, fourth or fifth, in free rhythms at the speed of slowish declamation, they are thus 'earthed'. Mompou effects his familiar equation between spirit and flesh, though the more personally transcendent, less traditional, approach of the words encourages him to a tauter harmonic acerbity, and to more far-ranging tonal excursions, if not modulations. Having set off in white note C major, with a IV V I progression which the bass momentarily flattens, the music finds its way to aeolian E minor, which turns into ionian G major. This is abruptly switched to G minor: from which point the homophony, slowing down, meanders flatwards, grows chromatic, and lands in a remote — but for the moment unequivocal — D flat major. The final section, returning to tempo primo, evokes *silencio eterno*, using chromaticism to release us from, rather than to affirm, sensuality. The theme wriggles serpent-like before clearing to its original, lucently ionian C major: which makes emotive sense since the Christian serpent proved an agent for redemption. The oscillating chromatics in the words *Vivir oscura humilde cenicienta* hint at supernatural mysteries in a way that recalls not only early Messiaen, but also early Maxwell Davies, in his settings of medieval carols, though this is not an 'influence' but a consanguinity of mind.

Le Jardin Retrouvé

Mompou's final bars are, however, more naively positive than the French or British composer dare be, for his consummatory cadence modulates from ionian C to its equally unsullied dominant, G major: wherein *Y soy tu eterno amor para quererte*.

Yet the core of Mompou's religious heart is not here, but in the extraordinarily simple setting he made of part of St John of the Cross's sublime *Cantar del Alma*. It exists in two versions, one for his basic voice and piano, the other for chorus and organ, both dated 1951. The religious dimensions of the images of water, night and sleep that haunt all Mompou's music are given, in St John's words, explicit mystical formulation: 'the eternal fountain is hidden, though I know well where it hides And it is of the night . . . This living fountain that I long for, in this bread of life I see it And it is of the night'. The text is set, in the voice and piano version, *dans le style grégorien*, unmeasured, in the aeolian mode on E, and is sung entirely monodically. Though Mompou's piano does not intrude into this divinely im-personal oneness, he does offer a measured ten-bar prelude, interlude, and postlude before, between, and after the stanzas. This piano music is scored (like the comparably *cantiga*-like movements from the Songs and Dances) in four quasi-singing parts, identical with the choral version except for slight modifications of range. The first three bars undulate tranquilly over a tonic E as pedal; slowly the bass moves melodically, and extra parts emerge to incorporate a dominant ninth and a still more emotive dominant thirteenth: which leads, by way of a weeping augmented fifth, back to E minor. These ten bars, in achieving equilibrium between horizontal melodies and vertical harmonies, are quintessential Mompou: traditional liturgical music, folk lament, and his individual sensibility have become one:

Mompou, the Church, and 'La Soledad Sonora'

And just as Mompou's ten bars of piano music never overlap with the quasi-divine incantation of St John, so they remain themselves inviolable. Heard three times, they are never minutely changed, except for the addition of a gong-like E at the end. Clearly this music concerns Mompou's intimate relationship to his God; clearly this is the experience incarnate in the very private music he has composed for his own solo piano and has published, under the title of *Música Callada,* in four books of short pieces dated 1959, 1962, 1965 and 1967. These pieces form a spiritual diary of his inner life during his later years, complementing the more social-communal diary of his Songs and Dances.

A link with the St John of the Cross song is manifest in the title, on which Mompou comments in his preface to the first volume:

> Il est assez difficile de traduire et d'exprimer le vrai sens de Musica Callada dans une langue autre que l'espagnole. Le grand poète mystique, San Juan de la Cruz, chante dans une de ses belles poésies: 'La Música Callada, la Soledad Sonora', cherchant à exprimer ainsi l'idée d'une musique qui serait la voix même du silence. La musique gardant pour soi sa voix Callada, c'est à dire 'qui se tait' pendant que la solitude se fait musique.

Le Jardin Retrouvé

Although St John speaks from a very ancient tradition of Christian mysticism, this experience is not dependent on traditional faith: a point worth making because it helps to explain why we, in Britain or wherever in the 1980s, may find such music deeply affecting. From a very different tradition, closer to us, another literally reclusive artist, the New England poet Emily Dickinson, 'had a terror since September I could tell to none; and so I sing, as the boy does of the burying ground, because I am afraid . . . My family are religious, except me, and address an eclipse, every morning, whom they call their Father . . . You ask of my companions. Hills, sir, and the sundown, and a dog as large as myself, that my father bought me. They are better than beings, but do not tell; and the noise in the pool at noon excels my piano'. Still more pertinently we may evoke another New Englander, Henry Thoreau, who wrote from his Edenic pool at Walden:

> As the truest society approaches always near to solitude, so the most excellent speech finally falls into silence. Silence is audible to all men, at all times, in all places. She is when we hear inwardly, sound when we hear outwardly. Creation has not replaced her, but is her visible framework and foil. All sounds are so far akin to Silence that they are but bubbles on her surface, which straightway burst, an evidence of the strength and prolificness of the undercurrent . . . In proportion as they do this, and are heighteners and intensifiers of the Silence, they are harmony and purest melody.

Such audible silence calls for special proclivities of mind and sensibility, and also for an awareness of time and space such as Thoreau had in his 'New Hampshire everlasting and unfallen, with dew on the grass'; and such as Mompou recaptured, a century later, in both rural and urban Catalonia.

If Mompou's spells and games reflect man's age-old attempts to escape from or to conquer his solitude, his *música callada* is his acceptance of it. In the still, small voice of silence he becomes one with solitude, as his piano *becomes* 'the noise in the pool at

Mompou, the Church, and 'La Soledad Sonora'

noon'. In the process he creates a sound that has not been heard in music before: which is obviously a rare achievement. All the pieces are short, most are slow and soft; all use non-developing phrases that might be called aural 'gestures' – of voice, arms or body – but are also melodies. The harmony is extremely chromatic: so much so that tonality is not always established, though the music is not a-tonal. At the same time this chromaticism is very different from that of Mompou's 'European' works such as the Chopin Variations. The 'pre-historic' magic of the early pieces seems to have alchemically metamorphosed the sensuality of Mompou's naive romanticism, creating harmonic textures that, although sensuous, are tart. If chromatic harmony be traditionally associated with expressivity and sometimes with emotional indulgence, here it is not less sensual but more austere. The typical Mompou nostalgia and regret are no longer pertinent, for *these* moments are outside time and space. The sounds are deeply pentrative, of soul rather than of body; and the sexual-religious metaphor is as appropriate here as it is to St John of the Cross himself, to St Theresa, and to a long sequence of 17th century mystically erotic poets of whom Richard Crashaw is merely the most extravagant English representative. Interestingly enough, Crashaw was well versed in Spanish as well as Italian theology and devotional poetry.

The features of Mompou's *Música Callada* referred to above do not, however, typify the first piece of the first book, for Mompou introduces his private muse from the porch of ecclesiastical tradition. The piece is marked *angélico*, and lives up to it, being a gentle aeolian incantation accompanied by little bells pentatonically ringing on A, B and D. The incantation is played twice, first time finishing with the mode transposed to E, the bells silenced as two additional lines mould the cadence. The music has modestly effected a transition from angelic or child-like rune to modally religious polyphony. Bells return for the da capo, and the part-writing in the approach to the cadence stays in aeolian A. The white note texture passes through a tenderly dissonant suspended seventh before the bare fifth

Le Jardin Retrouvé

(God's interval) is attained from the major second above, the flat seventh below:

If this is a distillation of previous Mompou musics, with the second and third pieces he enters the hermetic world of his Silent Music. He makes the point verbally in quoting Valéry: *Car j'ai vécu de vous attendre Et mon coeur n'était que vos pas*, the *vous* presumably being God. The tiny second piece — most of them are one page, none more than two pages, long — tells us that Mompou's God is not always *angélico*. A 'cry' of dissonantly related parallel sixths droops in painful appoggiaturas, answered by a more lyrical gesture, also in dotted rhythm, with quasi-canonic dialogue:

Both phrases are repeated, screwed up respectively a tone and a fifth. The piece disperses in the rocking sixths, with a *profond* gong-bell on a low pedal E.

In contrast to this small anguish — which does hint, however distantly, at St John of the Cross and even at the contorted forms of El Greco — the third piece is marked *placide*: appropriately, in that its E flat major *tune* simply and symmetrically alternates

Mompou, the Church, and 'La Soledad Sonora'

an arpeggio with a flowing scale. Yet the harmony is oddly awry: the B flat major triad is compromised by a G flat in the bass, which generates a whole-tone scale leading to problematically enharmonic notation; the innocence of the tune is disorientated:

We have met this blend of wide-eyed wonder and startlement before in Mompou's music, though never with such sharp lucidity. And the fourth piece, marked *aflitto e penoso*, is even more 'afflicted' than the second, for it is still built from weeping double appoggiaturas in parallel thirds, fourths and fifths, dissonantly grinding over a moving bass. A da capo adds a fourth part to the original three, creating tritonal chords that paradoxically sound both stark and ripe. The music does not establish tonality until its final cadence, when the appoggiatura thirds subside on to E minor.

No. 5 calls on an ostinato of regularly repeated quavers to induce trance. Although this reminds us of his early magic pieces, the directive *legato metallico* indicates that here the texture is not *dreamily* hypnotic. The repeated notes, oscillating between B flat and A flat, accompany a swaying incantation in parallel sixths, sometimes notated as augmented fifths. The B flats become fifths on E flat: in which key the chant rings more harshly, in chords built from Mompou's familiar fourths. A coda shifts the pendulum from triple to duple time, bells tinkling steelily in a chord telescoping the harmonies of the chant and of the ostinato. But the next piece is prevailingly melodic; an arching melody aspires upwards from E through the lydian sharp fourth and sixth, then falls through two fifths. A drone on low E and B supports the song, though the answering clause, in which the theme is inverted, is modally polyphonic and freely canonic:

Le Jardin Retrouvé

The da capo alters the 'altered' notes, with an effect slightly distraught though never destructive of lyricism. There's a fade-out in an only implicitly resolved appoggiatura over a spread E minor triad.

No. 7 reverts to Mompou's magic vein, alternating a phrygian incantation on F, low in the bass, with rocking gestures in middle register. These telescope tonic, dominant and subdominant chords, thereby defusing the normal European means of progression – as does Stravinsky in his middle years. Though the answering clause flows more lyrically, in three parts, it goes nowhere, and returns to the rocking pendulum, outside time even as it measures it. The eighth piece might be a *Cant magic*, more rarefied. A small incantation of a drooping D major triad, with a tailpiece of scalewise falling fourth, is accompanied by a single bell-chord of E, C and F sharp. A coda lifts the incantation into the heights and sharpens the bells with tritones before fading on an A major triad with added notes.

The last number – unusually given a key signature, that of 'paradisal' E major – looks back to the songful no. 6, which was in E minor with phrygian overtones. Two, three and four part writing creates, from a melody swinging between fourth and fifth in slow dotted rhythm, a texture at once radiant and astringent; the first harmony note is a tritonal (lydian) A sharp. After a brief 'middle – more animated in its dotted rhythm,

Mompou, the Church, and 'La Soledad Sonora'

though the harmony still moves slowly if at all – the song is restated an octave higher. It disperses in an interlacing of fourths, fifths and sixths, and comes to rest in drooping appoggiaturas, through which the dissonant A sharp still tingles. In context, the added seconds and sixths of the final cadence no longer recall jazz pianism, but achieve ethereality through their sensuality:

Book I of *Música Callada* outlines the prototypes Mompou is to explore in the later books. In volume 2 the first piece (no. 10 in the series) seems to be triggered by the last piece from Book 1, since it is mostly in three voices interlaced in arpeggiated polyphony, around E flat minor but gravitating towards a dorian C minor. No. 11 is closer to Mompou's folk-style dances, but more abstractly idealized. The left hand has an ostinato alternating the fifth D to A with the ninth F to G; the duple rhythmed tune is in B flat. The middle section has the tune in the bass, bassoon-like, while the right hand has explosively percussive dissonances. Repeated in the treble, the 'bassoon' tune becomes bucolic piping, supported by open fifths. A strict da capo of the opening clause is rounded off with a slow coda resolving into B flat with added fourth.

If this delightful piece is a throwback to Mompou's folk-dance vein, no. 12 is a *cant magic* and a tintinnabulation of solemn bells, emulated by open fifths with added minor sixth, in hypnotically dotted rhythm. Secundal dissonances add acerbic overtones in the answering clause; a filigree of semiquavers garlands the repeat with tritones, while the bells boom in the dotted rhythm on low Fs. In the last statement the two hands enunciate the obsessive rhythm in chords a semitone apart. The effect is awe-ful, in the strict sense; and communicates a little of

Le Jardin Retrouvé

its starkness to the exquisite thirteenth number, though it is marked *tranquillo, très calme*. Here the melody is rune-like, with bells in false relation on G natural and F sharp (equalling G flat):

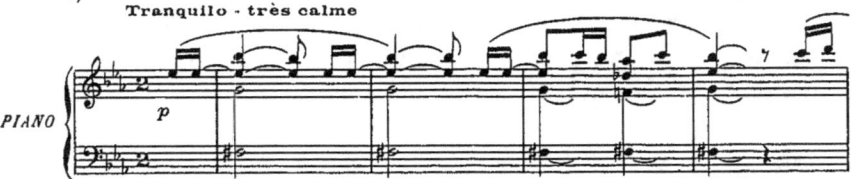

A middle section is suddenly *energico*, with trills and repeated notes punctuated by percussive dissonances. This doesn't, however, radically ruffle the 'pool at noon' of the first section, which radiantly returns, echoing on its fifth 'for ever and ever', as in the fairy tale.

But the fourteenth piece is no fairy tale, living up to its marking: *severo, sérieux*. Pervaded by the thrusting dotted rhythm that often betokens energy it has, for Mompou, powerful momentum, bounding into dissonantly secundal chords. Energy dissipates, however, in spread tritones, still in dotted rhythm, over a pedal C, the hidden tonic. The corporeal gestures of this piece don't affect its introverted nature; similarly the fifteenth piece, though built from a 'dislocated' appoggiatura over syncopated quavers, proves remote in effect from the emotive Chopin prelude it resembles. The second and fourth founded harmonies never quite coalesce with the weeping appoggiaturas, the harmonies grow gradually starker. The ultimate resolution on a D minor triad is as unexpected, yet as inevitable, as the A minor triad at the end of Chopin's second Prelude:

Mompou, the Church, and 'La Soledad Sonora'

The last piece in Book 2 (no. 16) is marked *calme*: deceptively so, for its fluttering semiquaver triplets create whole-tone frissons over the left hand's tolling bells, resonating through tritone, major seventh and minor third. A more songful middle section moves from three part polyphony to a folk-like repeated note tune, with astringent accompaniment. The piece fades into the ubiquitous tritone, so the piece remains elusive, even a bit illusory. Hermeticism characterises yet more strongly the third and fourth volumes, written during Mompou's seventies. No. 17, the first piece in volume 3, starts from the familiar slow dotted rhythm, in an E minor triad with added sharp fourth and seventh. The four-bar period is repeated a third higher, and rounded off with four more lyrical bars over a deep E pedal. This lyrical version of the obsessive gesture expands into an almost grand peroration, with fierce dissonances of second and seventh. These survive through the freely inverted answering clause, though it is marked *dolce*. A four-bar coda adds a rocking fifth to the original ostinato, and ends with added notes on an E minor triad. Far from being dreamy, these have the harmonic bite of Mompou's late manner, along with the mystery of his magic pieces. Though Mompou doesn't append notated question-marks, as he did in earlier works, questions still resound in the hermeticism of this very private music. This is evident in no. 18, which starts *luminoso*, with rocking triplets on A, B flat and F sharp, over a pentatonic ostinato. The melodic motif is a 'gesture' that asks an unanswered question: as does the pendulum movement of no. 19, which is ceremonial, though the rite is unconsummated, since what looks like a resolution into B flat minor turns into a sour dissonance over a drone on B flat:

Le Jardin Retrouvé

Nor is the twentieth piece as *calme* as its directive promises. Here too is a dotted rhythm pendulum which might be bells, the repeated note theme hovering over an undulating tritone and major seventh. The middle, in falling quavers, is riddled with false relations, and subsides into the repeated note ostinato with bell dissonances above it. Mompou's magic makes the end, when the ostinato rings on the fifth above a pedal D, seem inevitable, though there is little earlier intimation that tonality is rooted in or on D. The last piece in Book 3, no. 21, is more expansive and, in its double dotted rhythm, energetic. The rhythmic figure is tritonal, resolving on to a perfect fifth C to G, though the bass note is a cavernous, gong-like B. Tritones pervade the middle register, while aloft birds chirrup in minor thirds and triplets:

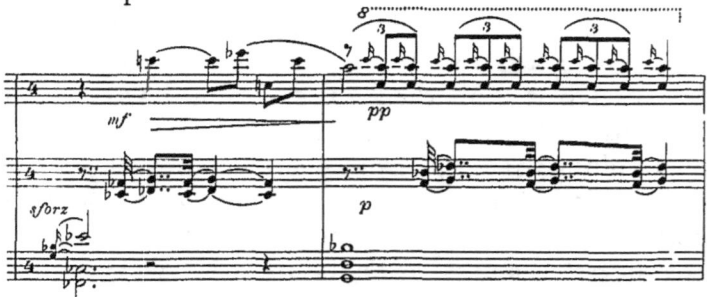

Key is undefined; false relations hint at bitonality. A da capo of the double dotted tritone motif reasserts, however, the deep-tolling B, which ultimately plummets to E.

The fourth volume, published in 1974 when Mompou was 81, carries his hermeticism to its most disturbingly beautiful point. No. 22 opens with the familiar bell-like repeated notes, this time syncopated. The two-note accompanying chords

Mompou, the Church, and 'La Soledad Sonora'

fluctuate between D minor and major, and between A major and C minor which might sometimes be E flat major. The phrase is repeated a fourth higher, followed by a song-like motif in cello register, aspiring upwards, vanishing in acute dissonance. An answering phrase, *molto cantabile*, begins on E flat, exquisitely cadences into G minor, and moves sequentially to a dominant seventh of D. A brief coda repeats the opening two bars but resolves them into D major, the repeated bell-notes echoing into silence:

This one-page piece indeed effects *multum in parvo*.

No. 23, *Calme, avec clarté*, is no less remarkable and still more original in sonority. Perhaps the most extreme example of Mompou's 'penetrative' dissonance, the piece is built from an initial rocking figure of swaying fifth F sharp-B over sixths that expand from minor to major, then contract. The tritonally based dissonances grow more acute as the tonality sharpens:

Yet the pain doesn't contradict the 'calm and clarity' the music generates, perhaps because of the lucent spacing. There is a

Le Jardin Retrouvé

philosophical and psychological as well as technical aspect of this: the saintly Spanish mystics saw pleasure and pain as interdependent. This may be latent in the twenty-fourth piece also, though it begins with muffled thirds over a bass oscillating between F, E flat and C: an obfuscating but not sharply dissonant sonority. Out of the obfuscation flowers a C major triad which is soon obliterated by three-part, flatwards tending undulations over neutrally fourth founded chords. In the da capo the luminous C major triad is sustained through a coda. A double appoggiatura echoes distantly and dissonantly: a memory of past pain that gives a slight fillip to present C major pleasure. The fluctuating quavers sound like one of Mompou's familiar images of water, which the C major triad illuminates with a shaft of sunlight:

No. 25 introduces another kind of 'rarefication': chords which became melody in being spread across the keyboard, with an effect very faintly reminiscent of that (to Mompou) totally alien tradition, Viennese serial chromaticism. Fourths perfect and imperfect, and major sevenths which embrace those two intervals, pervade the thin texture, until the wide-spaced 'gesture' is answered by a rocking figure in parallel fourths. There is no dialogue between this rune and the original gesture, but a simple co-existence. The still voice is heard in a still moment and peters out in unresolved dissonance which, since it doesn't seek resolution, seems not to need it. Philosophically, perhaps theologically, this is the point of *Música Callada* as a whole. The paradise it evokes had, of course, earlier been explored by Debussy, whose music likewise evades antecedence and consequence. Mompou's harder edges, however, make his paradise more uneasy. This may be attributable partly to his later date, partly

Mompou, the Church, and 'La Soledad Sonora'

to the fact that his God is an Almighty Father as well as sensuously Virgin Queen, whereas Debussy's god was pagan Pan.

No. 26 returns to the middle of the keyboard, and to wavering appoggiaturas in three parts, over a pedal C. The second eight bars introduce whole-tone and bitonal ambiguities, mounting to what might almost be called a climax on a dominant of A, but with G natural and B flat. The alternation of wavery waves and attempted progression is extended into sharper areas: only to subside, *molto lento*, in an exquisite passage of drooping thirds, the more affecting because the harmonies have previously been so tight:

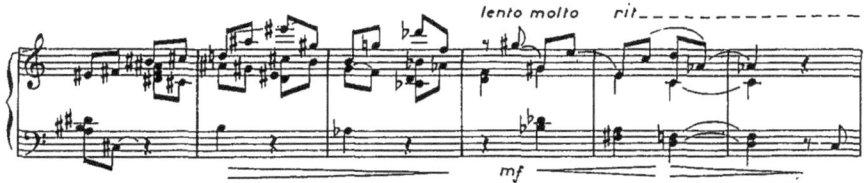

No. 27, *lento molto*, is arcane is the same sense as is no. 25, opening with telescoped chords of F major second inversion with G flat first inversion. These mysterious bells echo through a line of wide-flung quavers, merging into a self-rotating duologue:

These duple- and triple-rhythmed elements interchange at different pitches but without development: until a repeated-note melody in the dotted rhythm that pervades many of the pieces sings, *dolce e tranquillo*, over a pendulum triad of B flat minor. The magic bells penetrate the fadeout on the bare fifth: which is therefore not final after all.

But the last piece, no. 28, does attain a kind of finality. Beginning with slowly processional diatonic chords in C, it

Le Jardin Retrouvé

clearly recalls the ceremonial numbers in Mompou's earliest work, *Impresions Intimas*. The first four bars lead from C into aeolian E, and the clause is repeated, slightly modified, a tone lower. The next seven bars, growing more song-like by way of the familiar dotted rhythmed repeated notes, veer around aeolian B, the spacing growing more resonant. A brief middle at first chromatically interlaces versions of the dotted rhythm motif over syncopated dissonances; the passage seems to refer to, without strictly quoting, several of the song-style pieces from earlier Books of *Música Callada*. The return of the processional march is powerfully scored, with a sharp, B majorish flavour, in Debussyan organum though with acuter dissonances. Watery quavers return in 2 4, perhaps in retrospective reference to nos. 24 and 26. They flow into a da capo of the procession in its solemnly syncopated rhythm, beginning in C major again, again moving to aeolian E. In a coda, *molto rit.*, whole-tone added notes fall to an unambiguous, marvellously resonant C major triad: a 'final' consummation, with those original syncopated repeated notes now echoing in middle register on G:

The haunting effect of this music – especially when played by its dedicatee, the appropriately magical Alicia dé Larrocha – is out of all proportion to its apparently rudimentary, certainly minimal, means. One wonders, since Book 4 ends with so patent a reference back to Mompou's first work, whether he

Mompou, the Church, and 'La Soledad Sonora'

intended number 28 to be the conclusion of the cycle, and even of his life's work: which, at the age of ninety-three, would be fair enough.

Postlude:

Nature and Art in this together Suit;
What is most Grand is always most Minute.

WILLIAM BLAKE

THE modern adage that Small is Beautiful is singularly appropriate to Mompou; it might almost be said of him that small is beautiful, smaller more beautiful, and smallest most beautiful, for his one or two page spells and incantations on the whole 'do' more than his longer pieces in variation or rondo form, while the most concise of all his works — the fourth book of *Música Callada* — contains his most dense and emotionally complex music. Of course Mompou, in his 'green paradise of childish loves', does not attempt to grapple with contemporary realities, as do Schoenberg, Bartók, Stravinsky, Ives, Varèse, and possibly Carter, Boulez and Stockhausen. Yet his smallness is his significance, given the potency of his appeal. He makes the Moment sacred, doing within 'art' music what happens in magic spells, children's games, and intermittently in jazz and tribal pop musics — so that to deprecate the hints of demotic idiom that creep into his refined art is to miss the point. It is true that Mompou's games and festivities are heard from afar, *lointain*, recollected in tranquillity rather than actively indulged in. None the less his recollection, being pristine, rings true, and may effect small rebirths in us who listen.

Postlude

And it is possible to trace a slow evolution within Mompou's always unpretentious but not undemanding art. The early magic and childhood pieces, even those composed when he was little more than a boy, look *back* at, in order to re-create, the world of 'savages' and of small children; the folk song and dances look back at an agrarian society he loved but didn't belong to, though it became his, as he became its, in his music. In his Parisian works Mompou adapts 'Europe' to his *primitif* ends, learning in the process that Europe is part of his world: as is palpably true of his church music since its style is both traditional and modern, and the Church – for some people, certainly for Mompou – still lives. Without the artistic heritage of Europe, it is improbable that Mompou could have reached the ultimate stage of his *Música Callada,* in which the small pieces are magical moments that no longer need to be retrospective or nostalgic, since the spiritual verities they discover are timeless and solitary, within the heart of silence. Although the solitariness of this music is a-social, it is more than that to those who have learned to love it, since it tells us, in Thoreau's words, that 'through our recovered innocence we can discern the innocence of our neighbours'. Mompou's small music may have, in the context of the modern world, a religious significance deeper than we realize. Looking back at his spells, runes and incantations, entering into the solitary heart of his *Música Callada*, helps us to understand the wonderful words of Octavio Paz:

> Every moribund or sterile society attempts to save itself by creating a redemption myth which is also a fertility myth, a creation myth. Solitude and sin are resolved in communion and fertility. The society we live in today has created its myth. The sterility of the bourgeois world will end in suicide or a new form of creative participation . . .
>
> Modern man likes to pretend that his thinking is wide-awake. But this wide-awake thinking has led us into the mazes of a nightmare in which the torture chambers are

Le Jardin Retrouvé

endlessly repeated in the mirrors of reason. When we emerge, perhaps we will realize that we have been dreaming with our eyes wide open, and that the dreams of reason are intolerable. And then, perhaps, we will begin to dream once more with our eyes closed.

(The Labyrinth of Solitude 1959)

Highbury Fields,
LONDON,
July 30, 1985

NOTE

Mompou's early works were published by Union Musicale Franco-Espagnole or by Max Eschig, Paris. The bulk of his work is published by Editions Salabert, Paris: except for the Preludes, which are divided between Heugel, Paris, and Editorial Boileau, Barcelona.

The composer's complete recording of his piano music was issued in the seventies by Discos Ensayo, Barcelona, and distributed by the Musical Heritage Society, Oakhurst, New Jersey 07755, U.S.A. This original edition was deleted; but the recordings have recently been reissued on Compact Discs ENY 3418 and 3426.

Alicia de Larrocha's beautiful Mompou disc is still commercially available on Decca 410 287 1. Three discs of Mompou's piano music played by Pierre Huybregts are still available on Orion 76234, 78286 and 78310. Three of the songs from *Combat del somni*, sung by Nan Merriman, are available on a 1986 reissue of a recital of French and Spanish Songs in the HMV Treasury Series (EX 29 0654 3).

www.ingramcontent.com/pod-product-compliance
Lightning Source LLC
Chambersburg PA
CBHW071849230426
43671CB00012B/2121